VEHICLE
SCISSOR SKILLS
CHILDS NAME

Book Content

Remove the sheet along the trim line.

Color the image.

Cut out the image, using dashed lines.

Glue it into another book or hang the image.

Cutting Practice

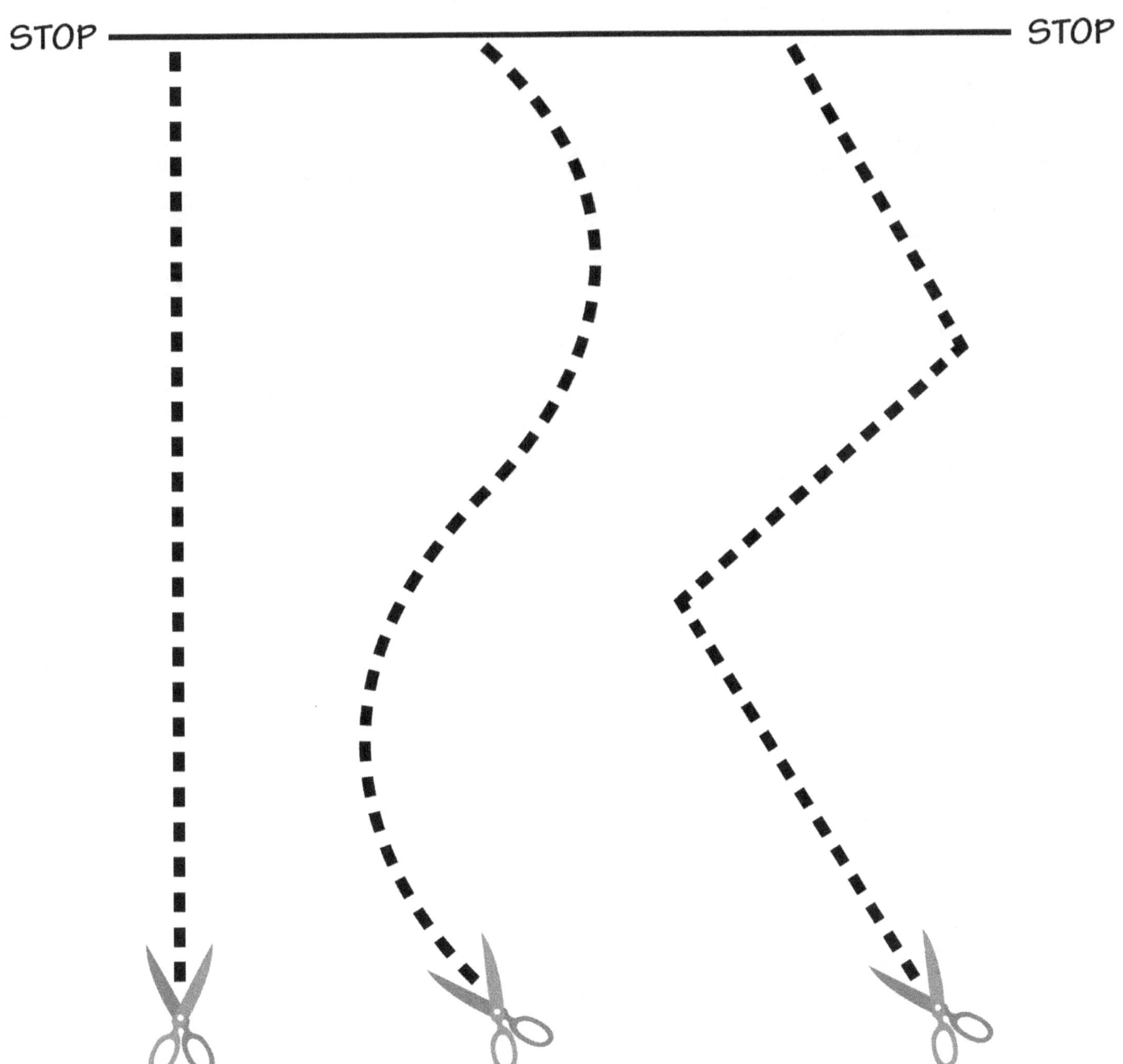

Let's cut
Color & Glue

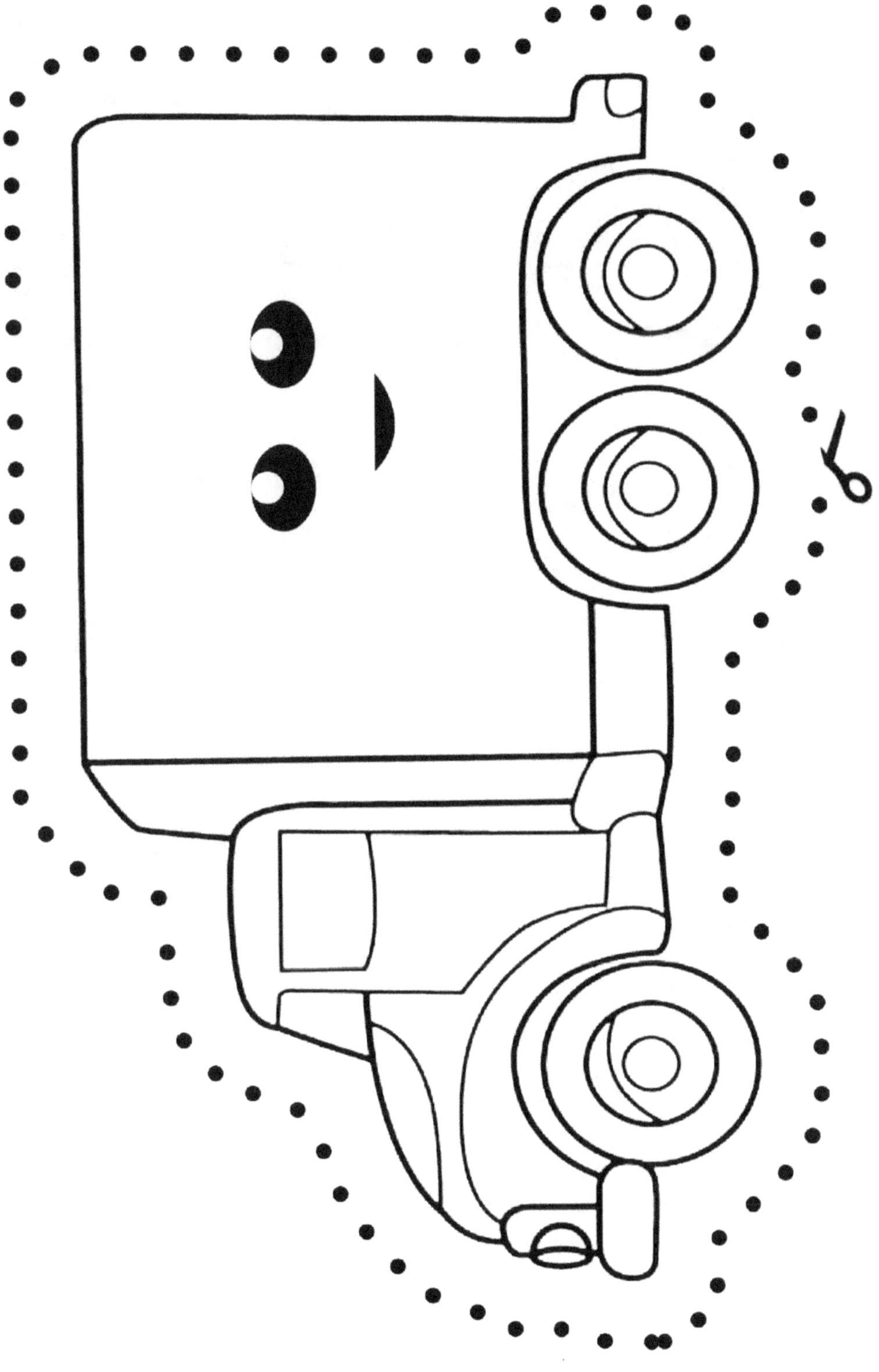

Let's cut
Color & Glue

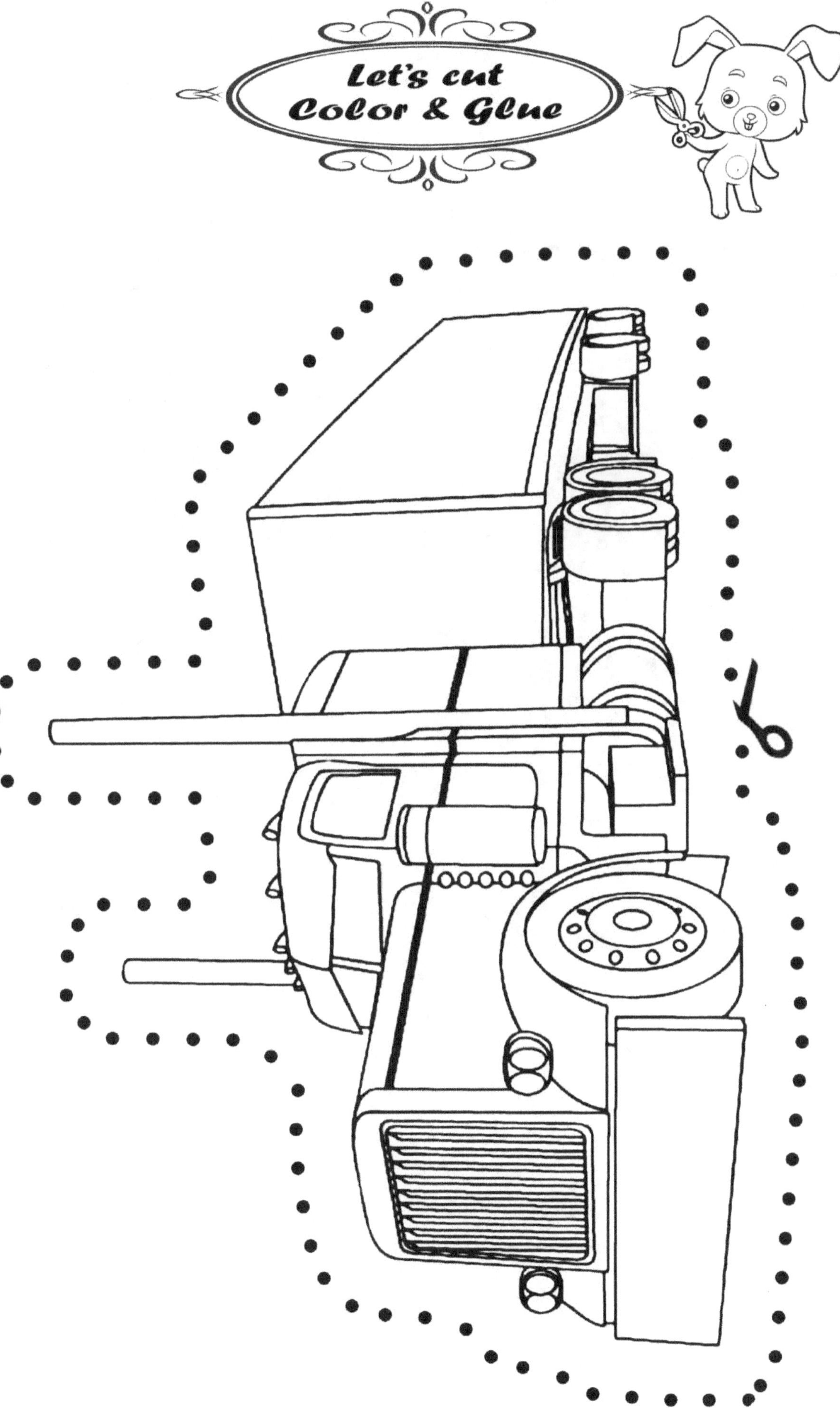

Let's cut
Color & Glue

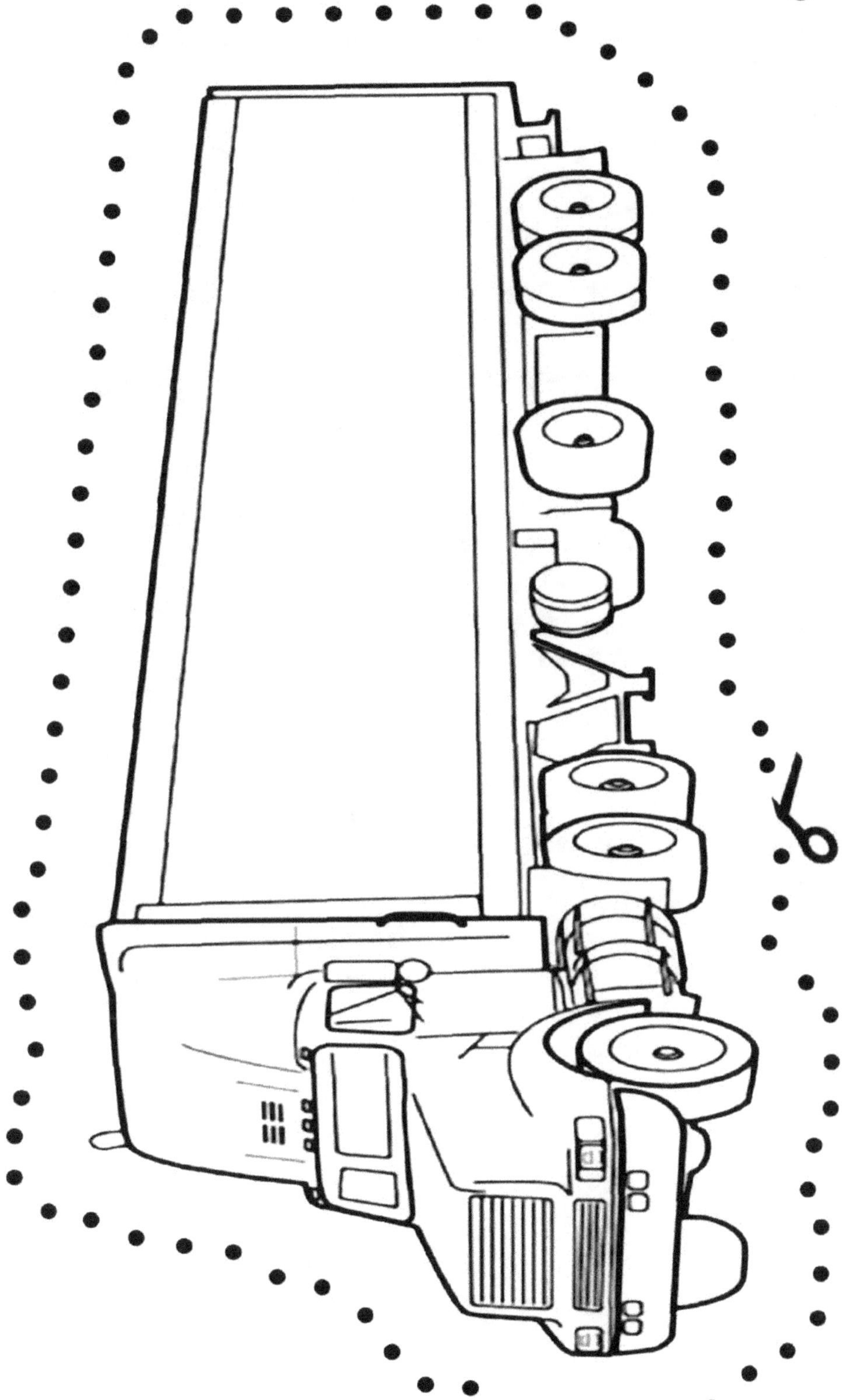

Let's cut
Color & Glue

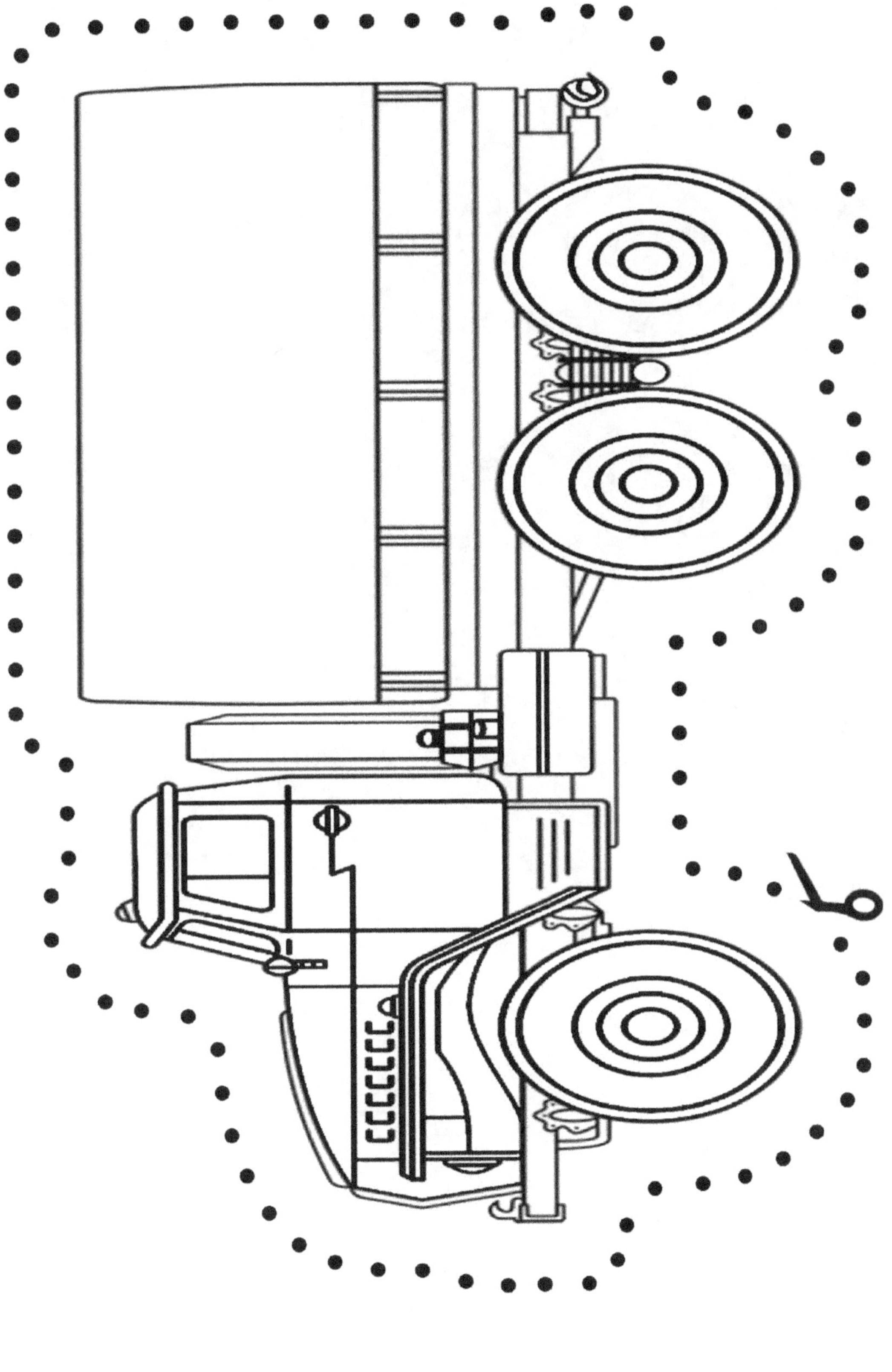

Let's cut
Color & Glue

Let's cut
Color & Glue

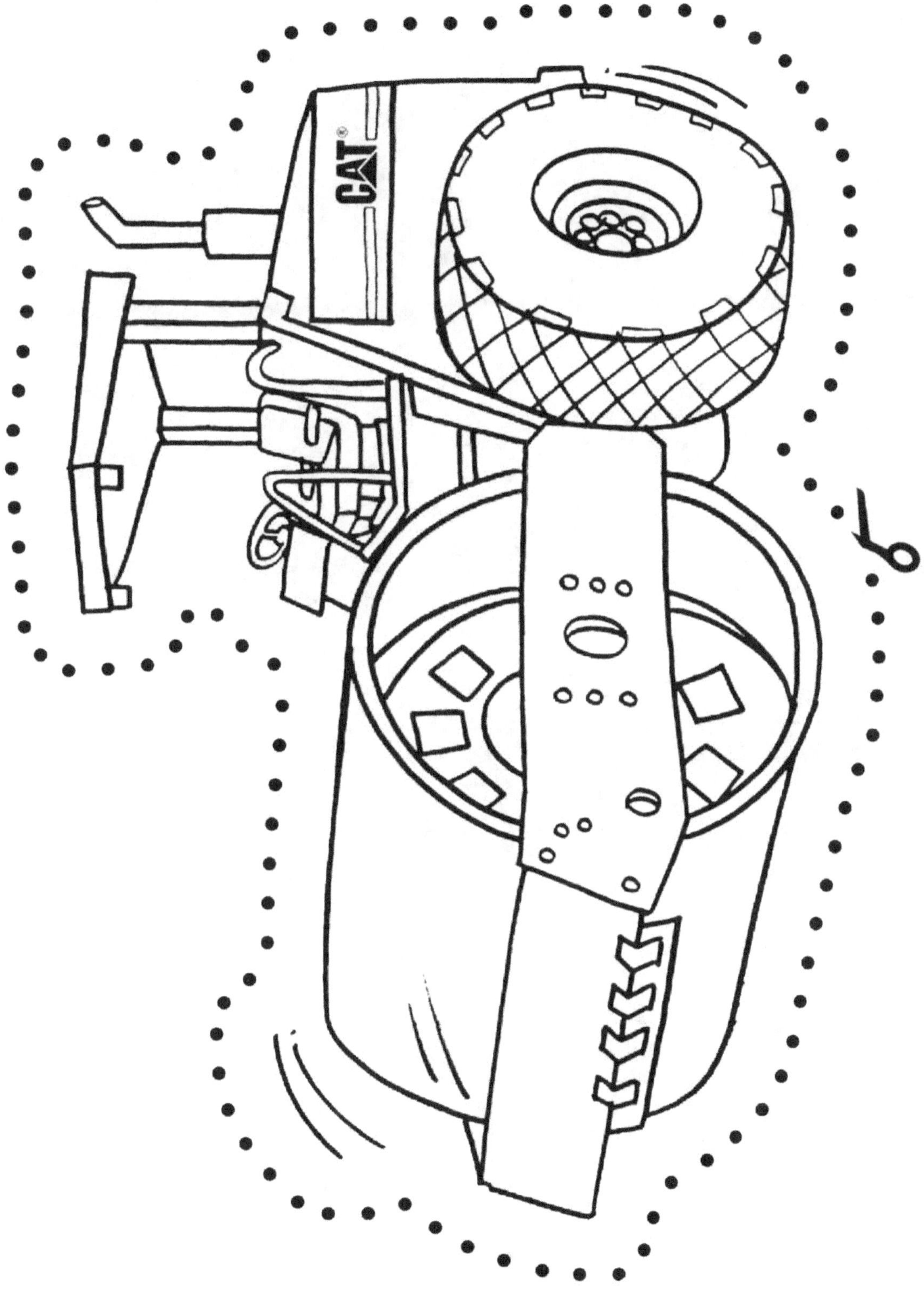

Let's cut
Color & Glue

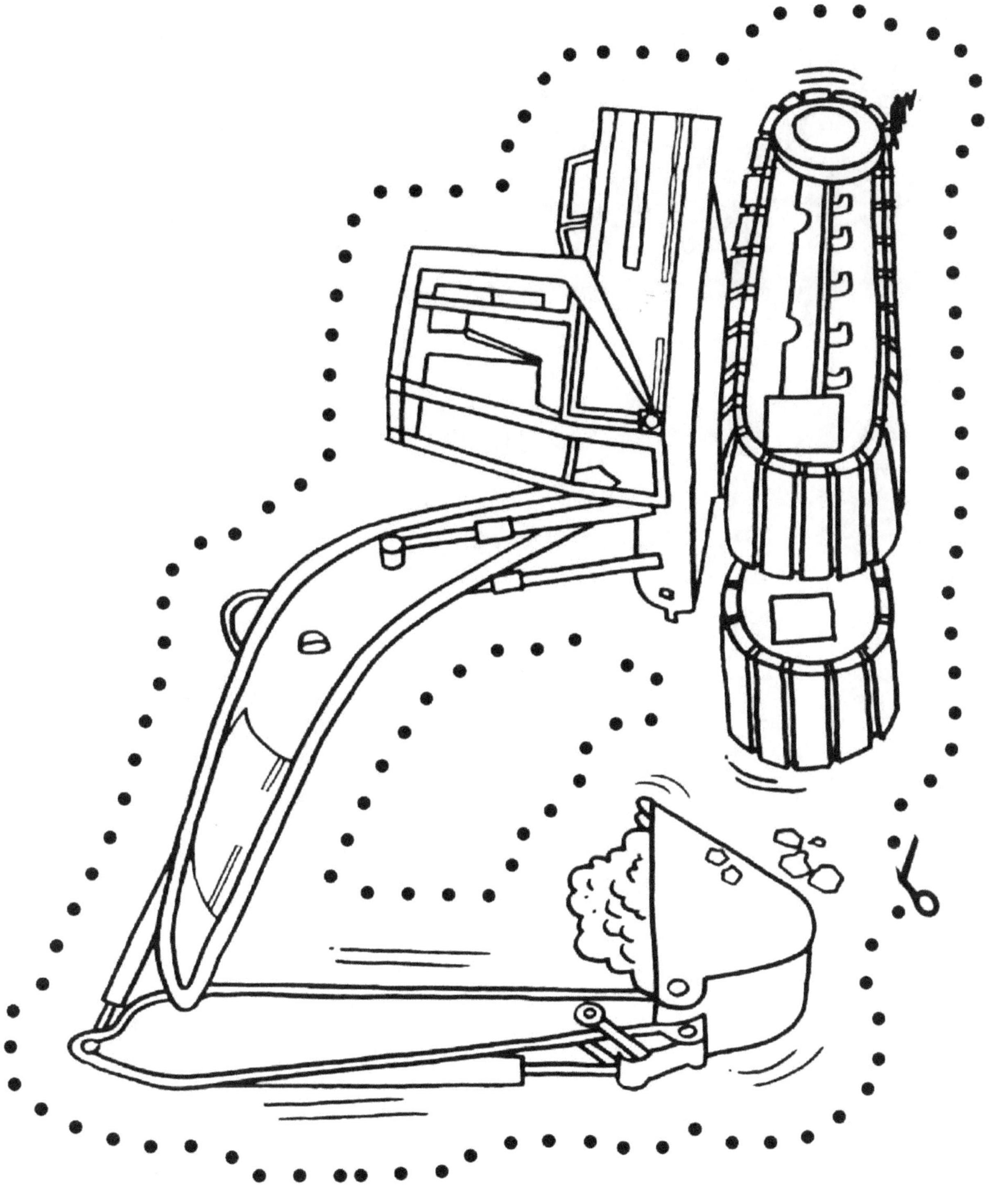

Let's cut
Color & Glue

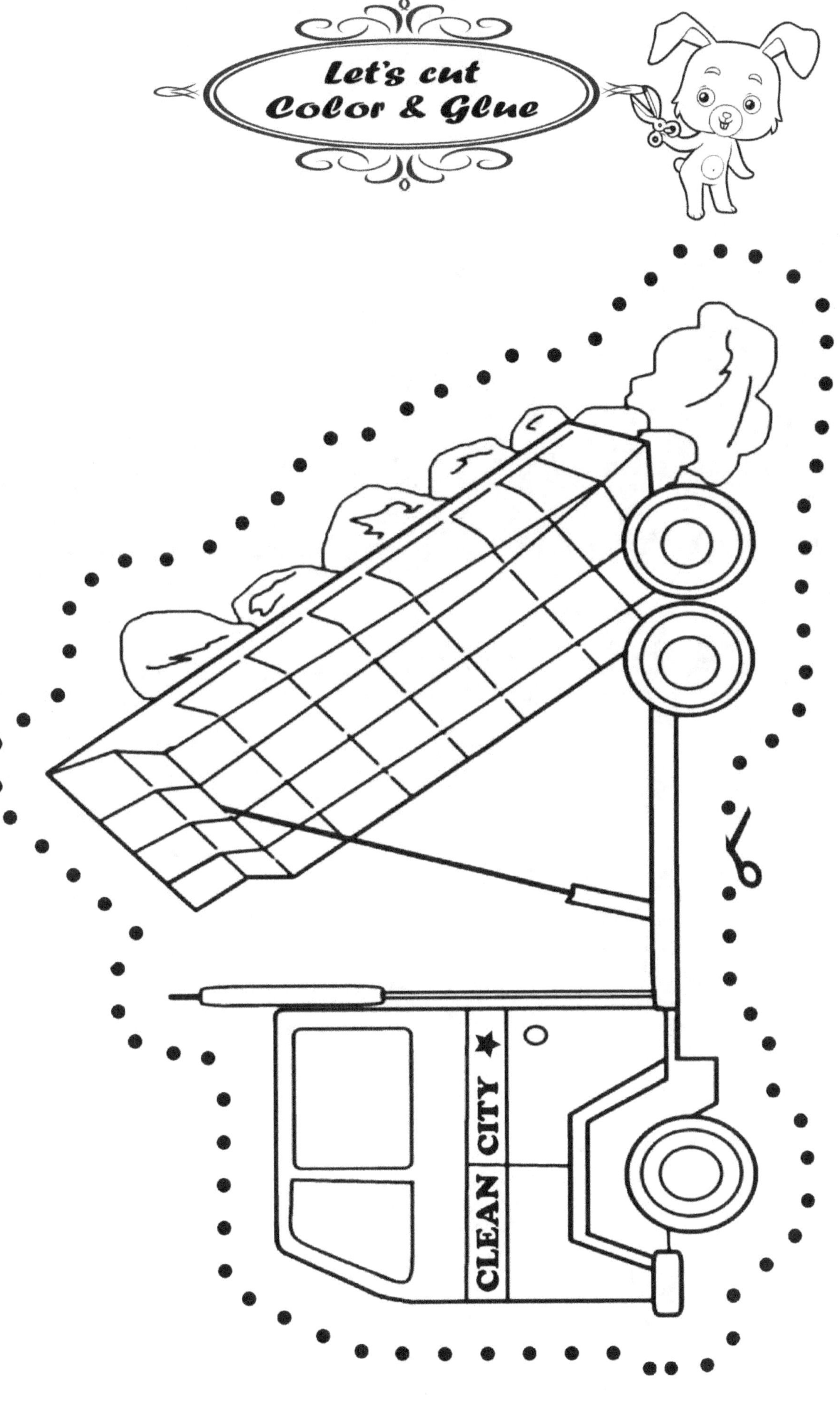

Let's cut
Color & Glue

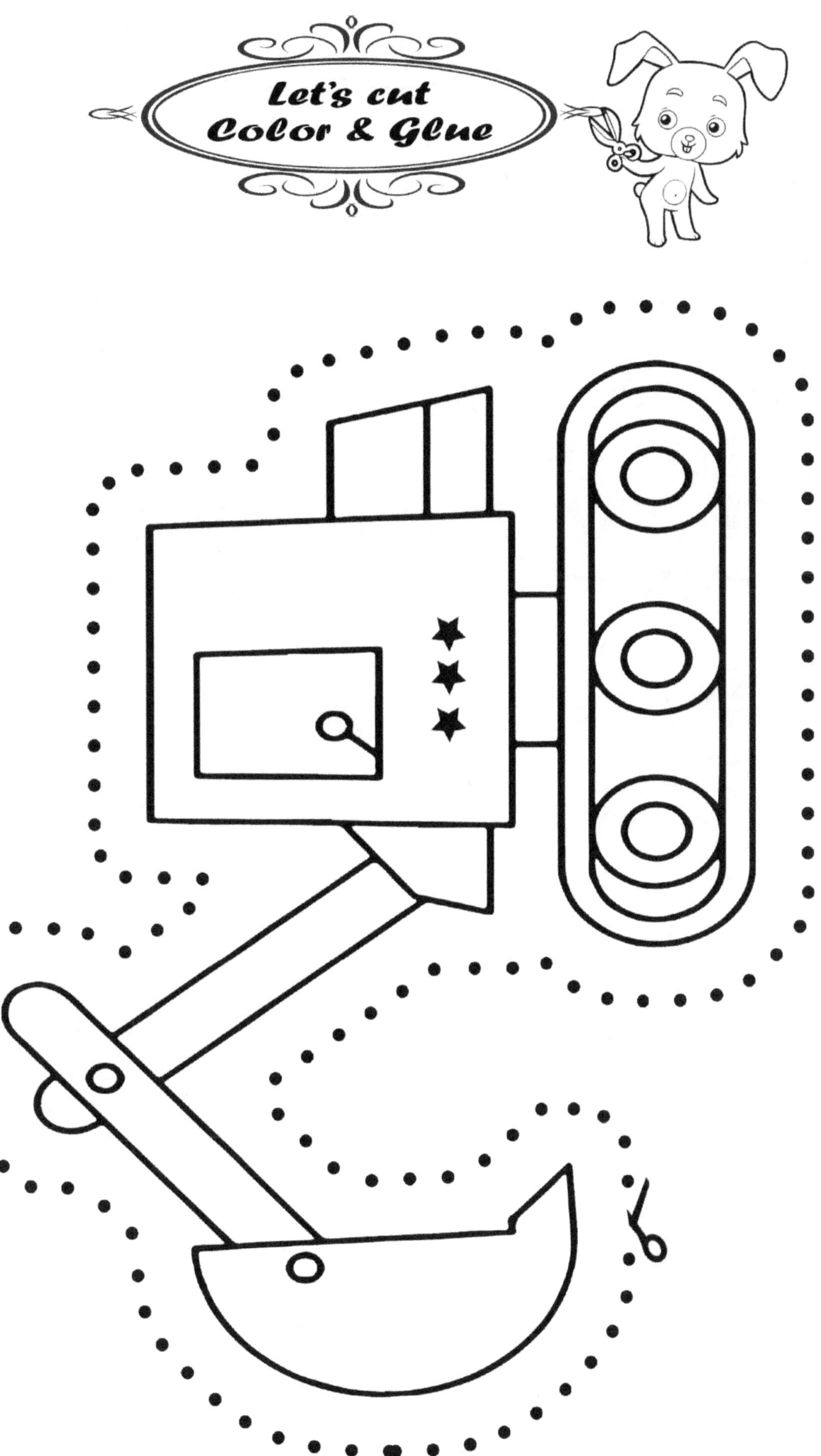

Let's cut
Color & Glue

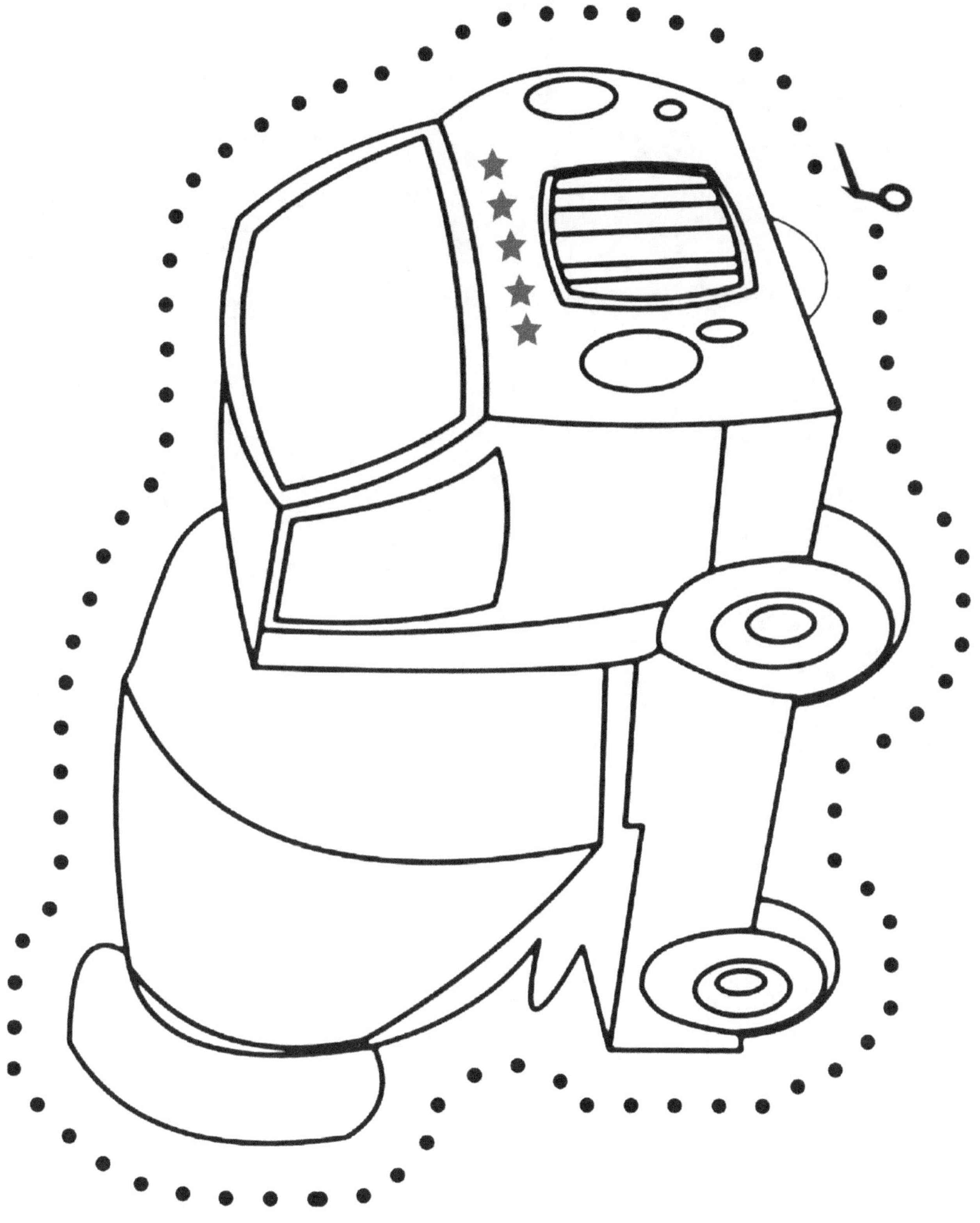

Let's cut
Color & Glue

Let's cut
Color & Glue

CITY

Let's cut
Color & Glue

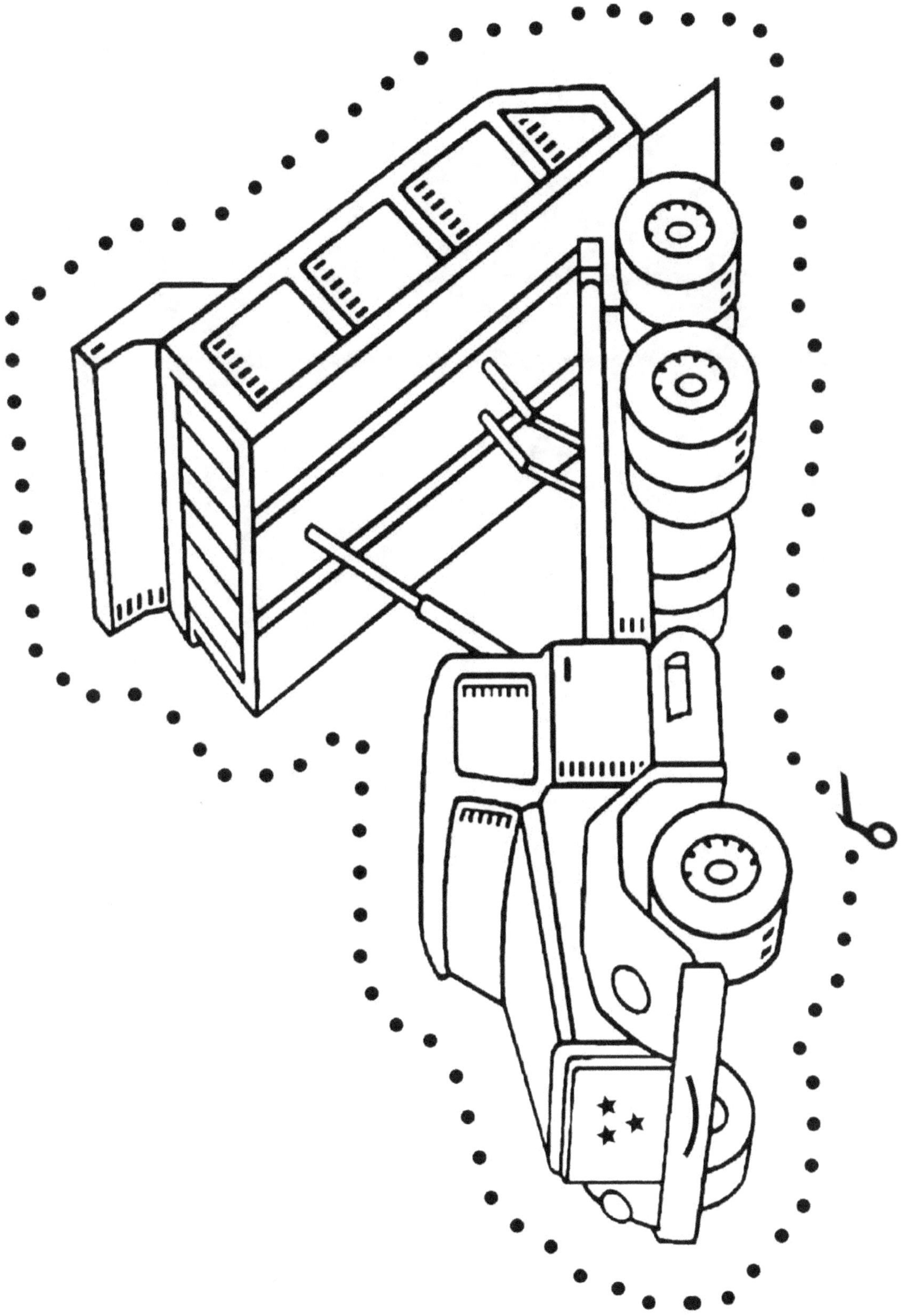

Let's cut
Color & Glue

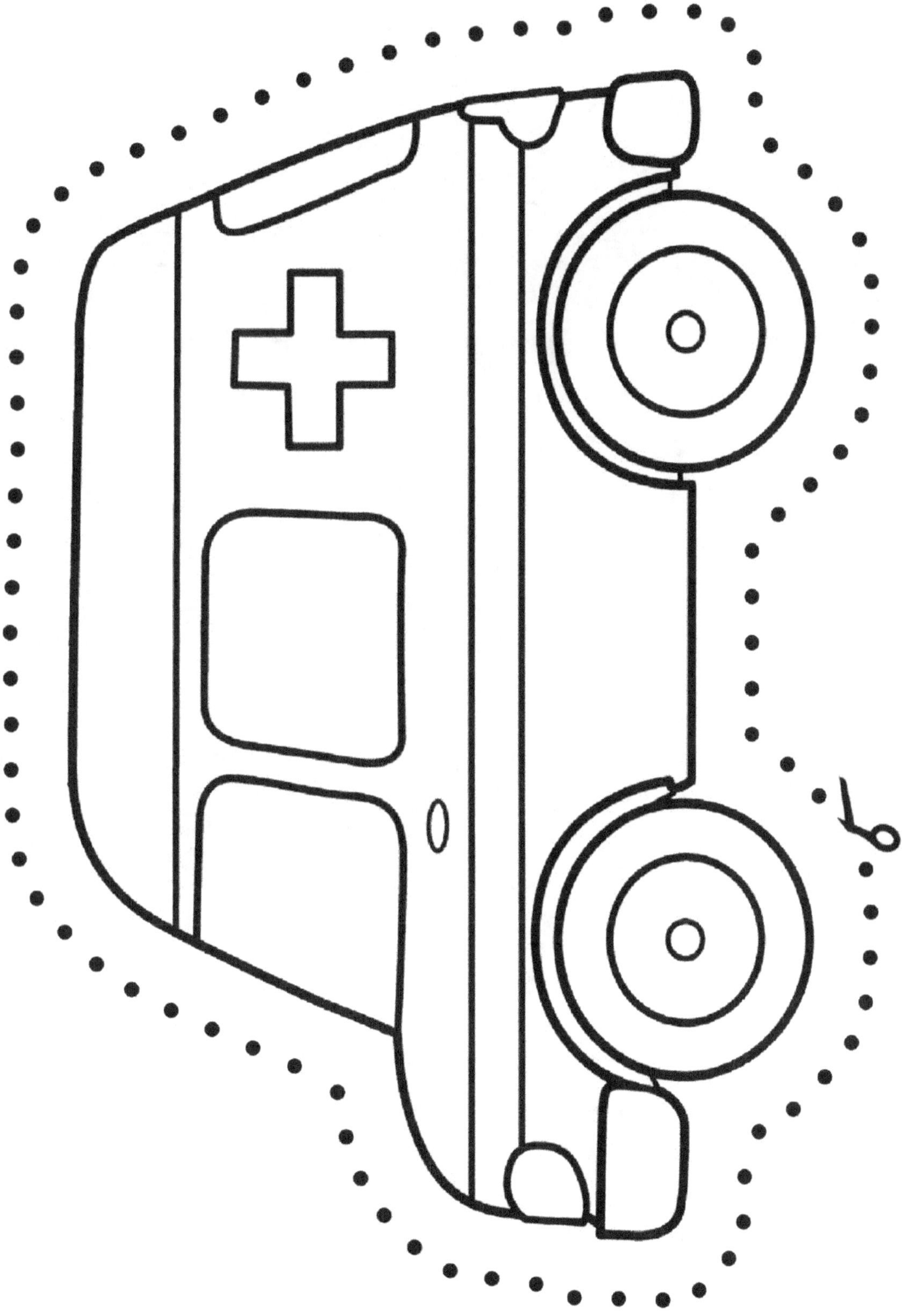

Let's cut
Color & Glue

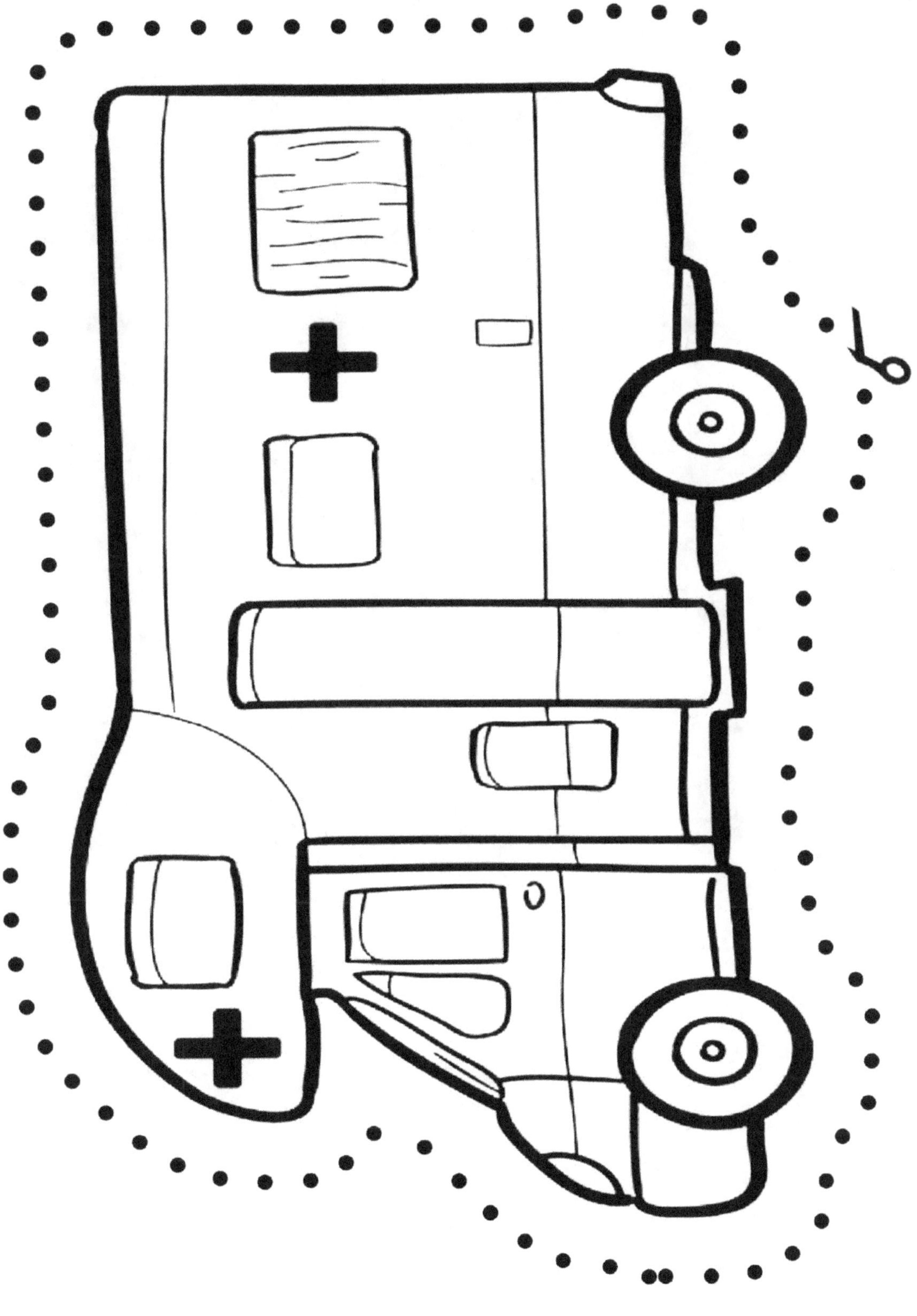

Let's cut
Color & Glue

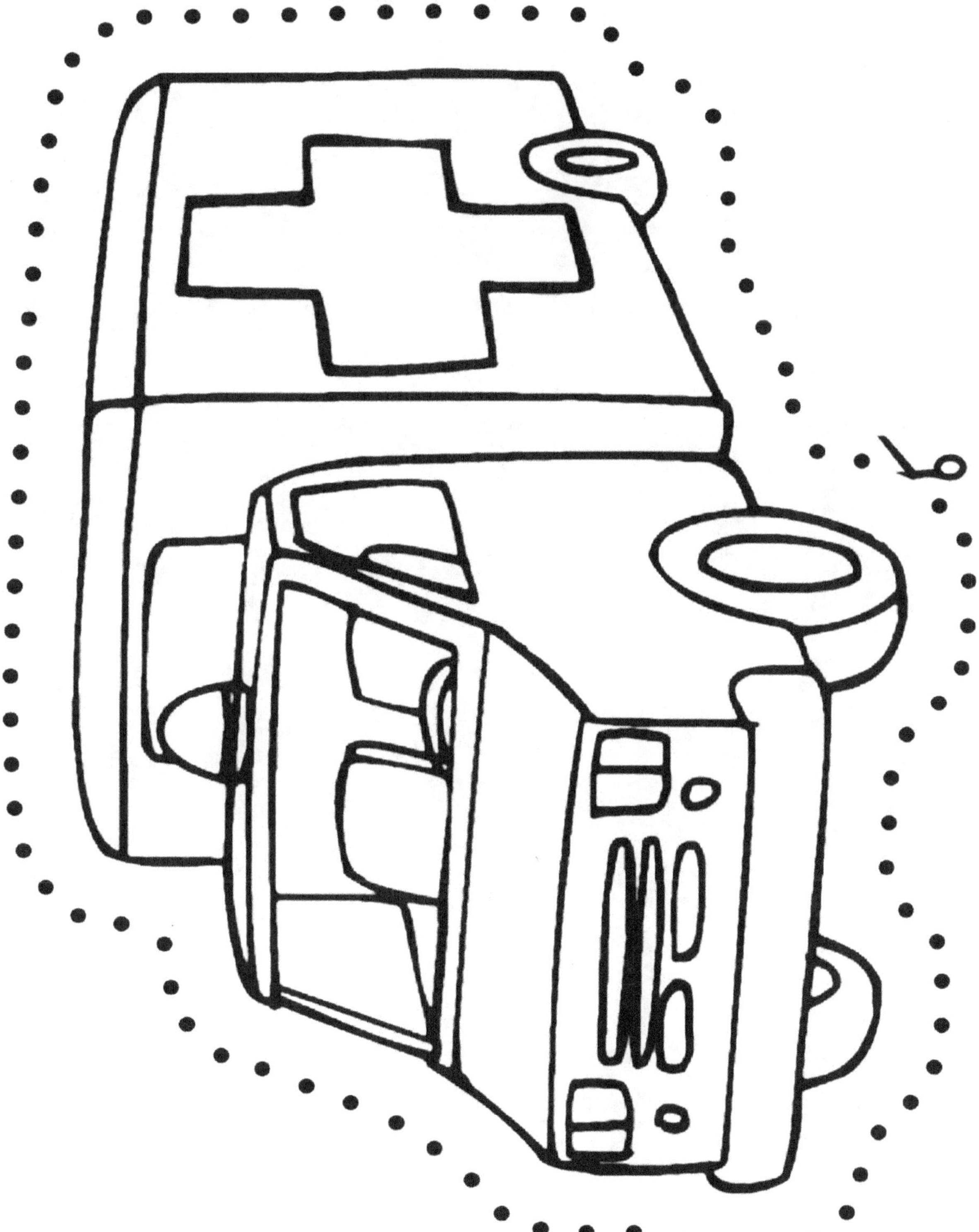

Let's cut
Color & Glue

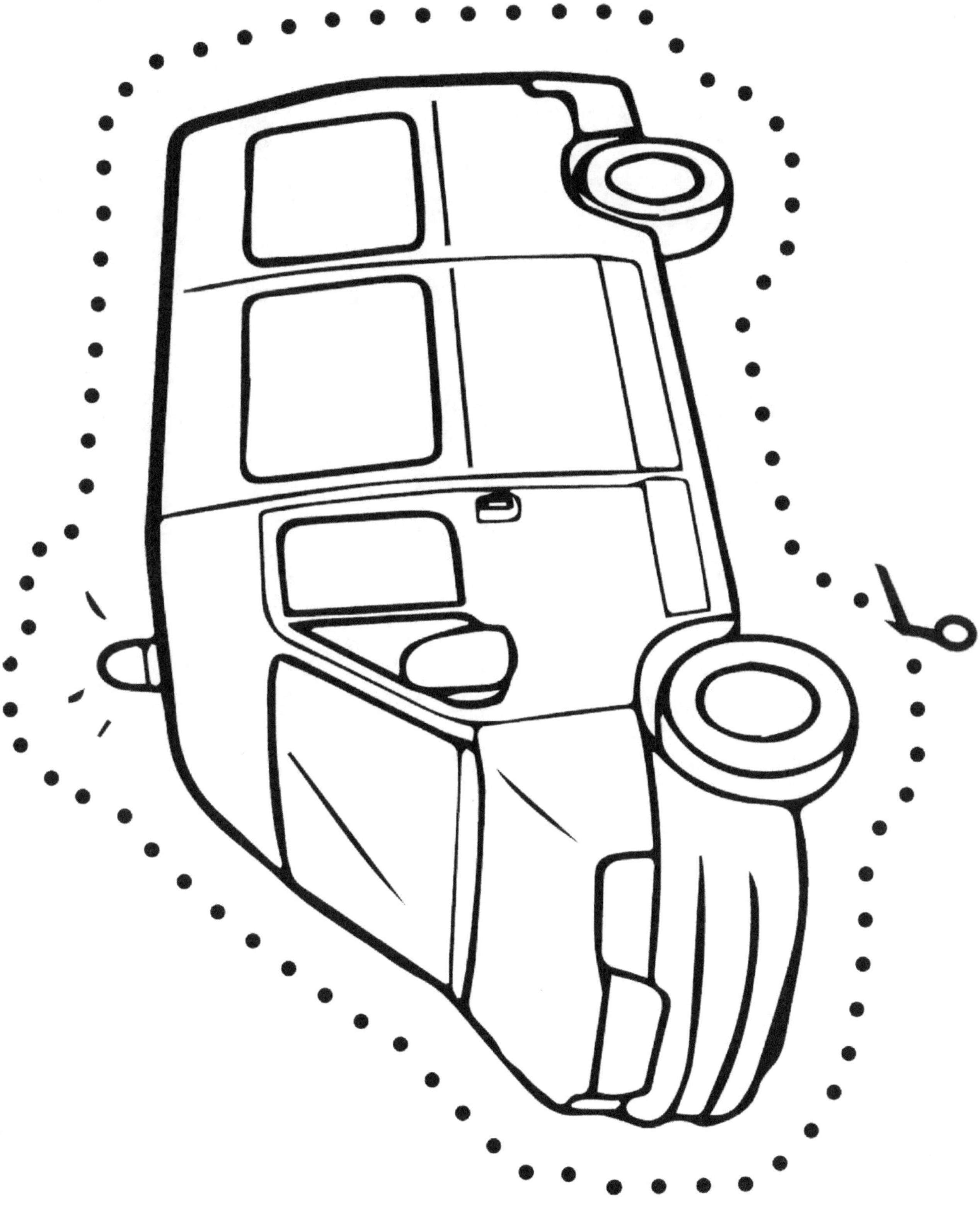

Let's cut
Color & Glue

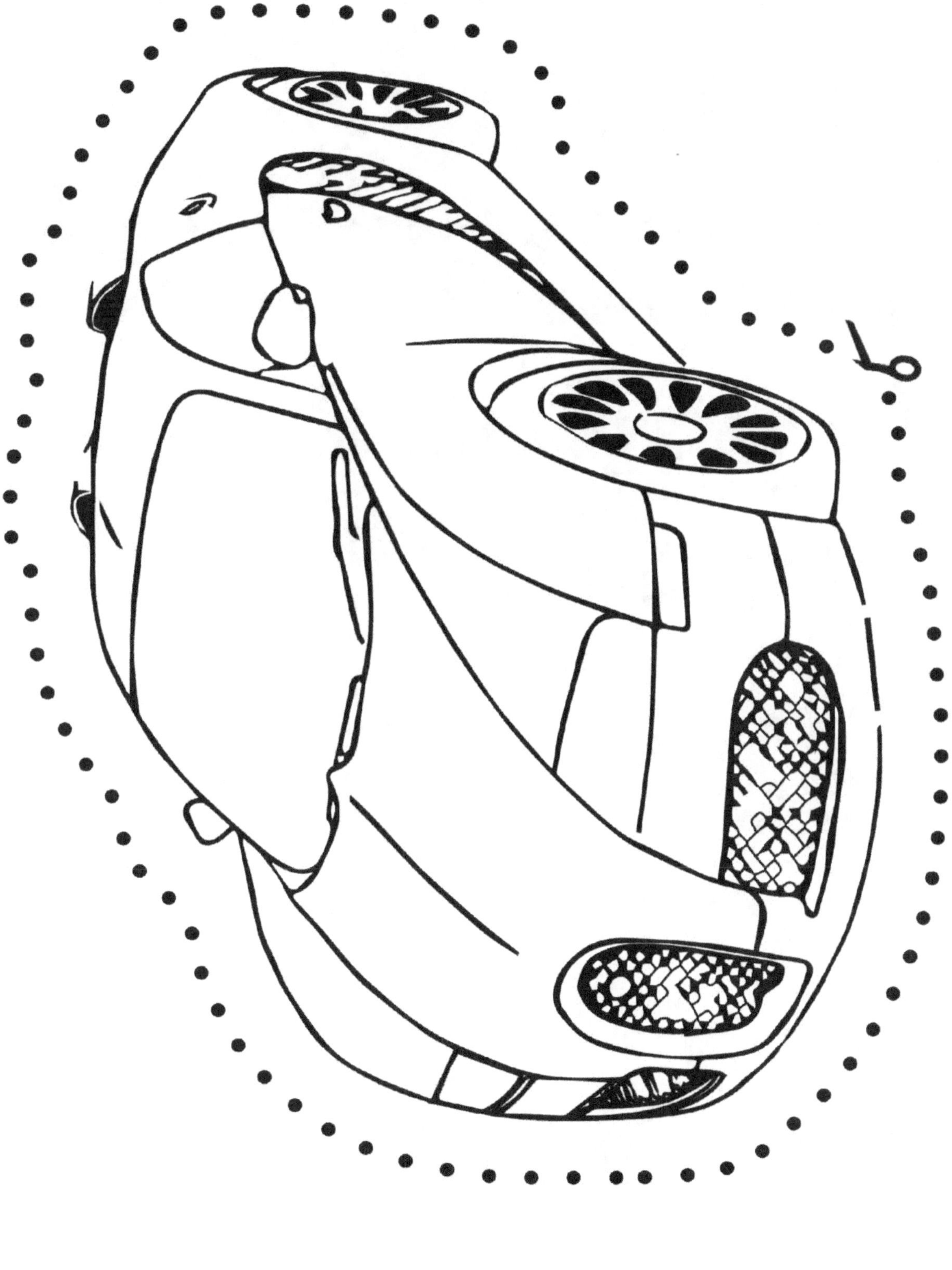

Let's cut
Color & Glue

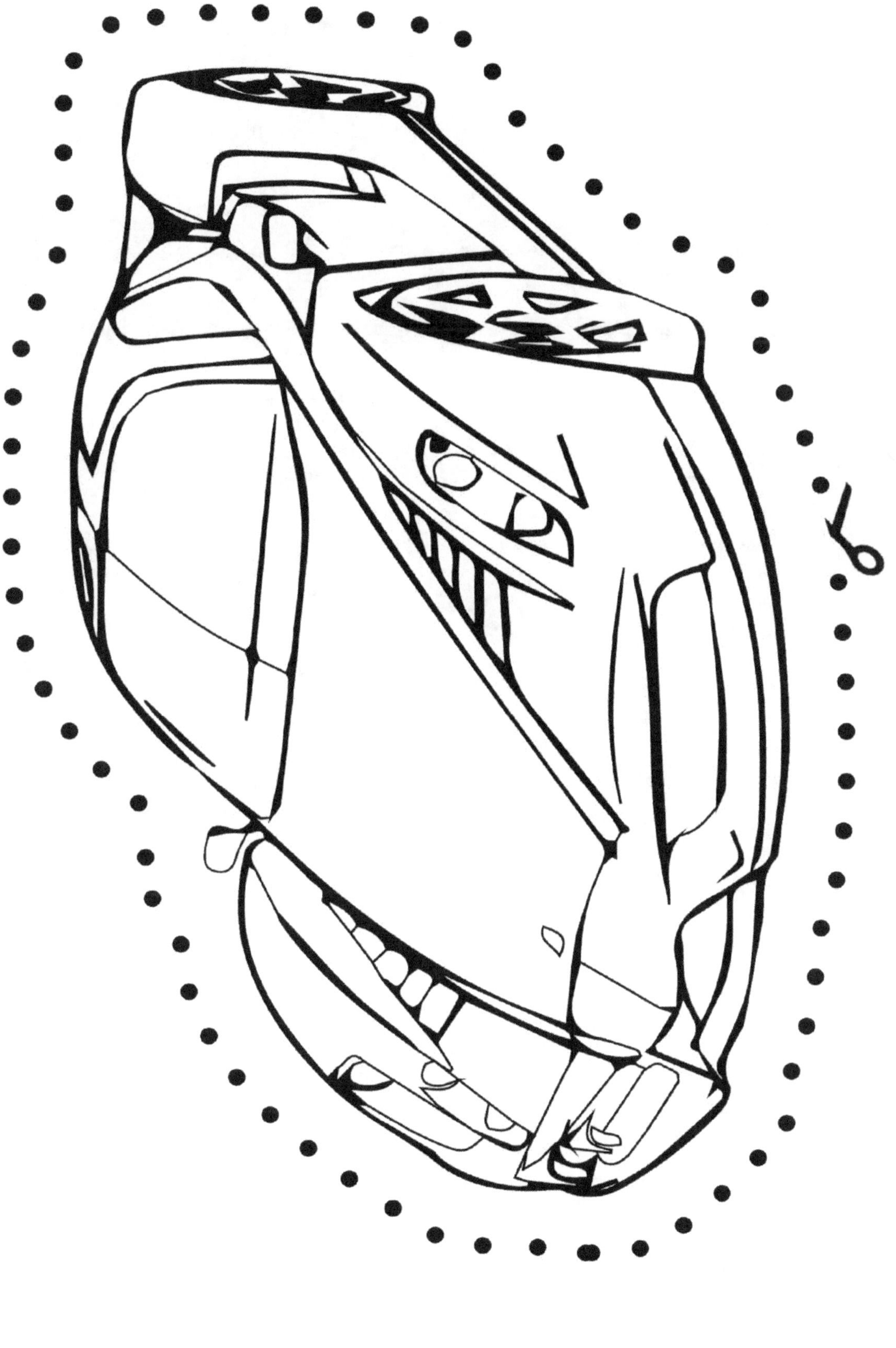

Let's cut
Color & Glue

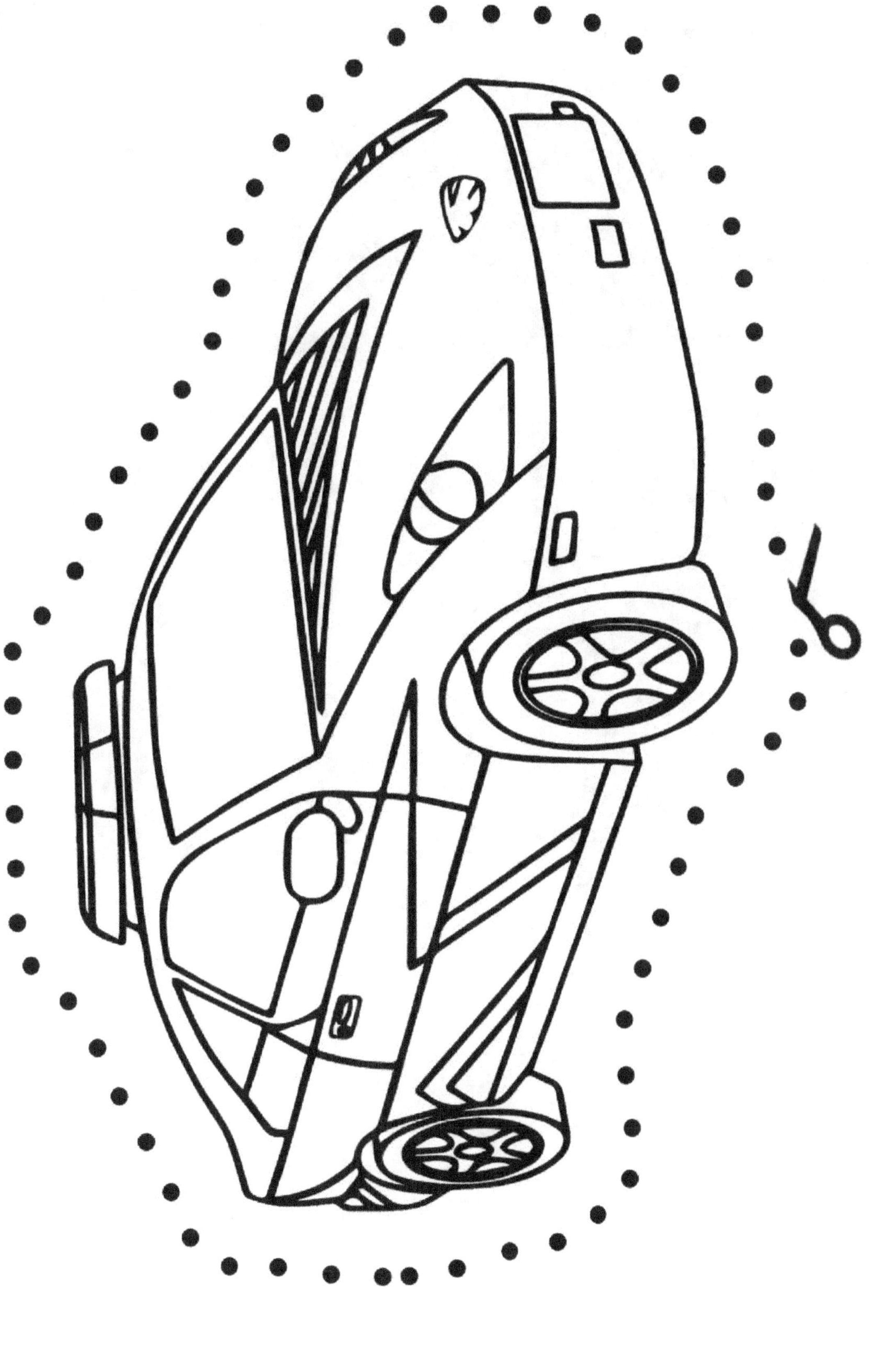

Let's cut
Color & Glue

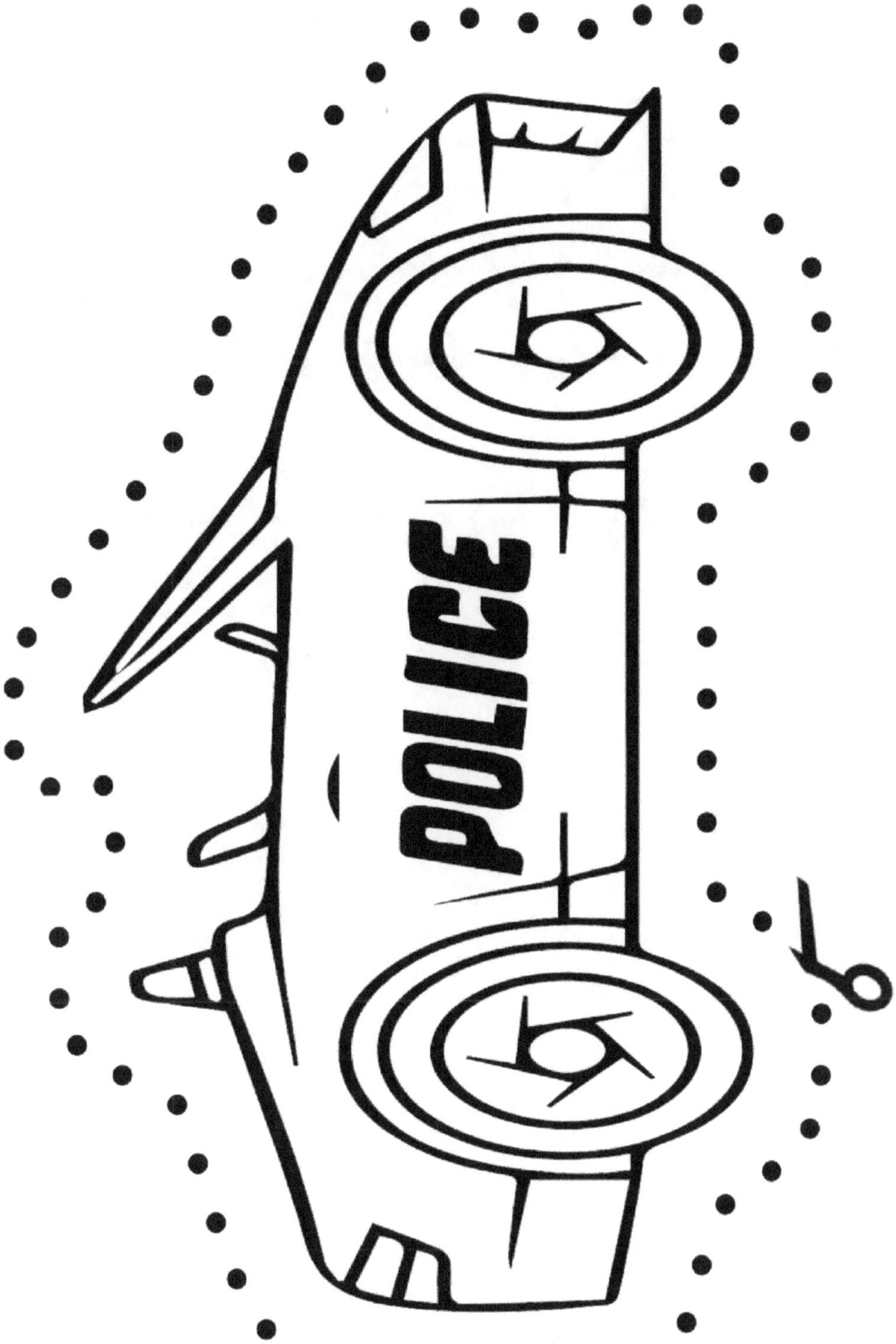

POLICE

Let's cut

Let's cut
Color & Glue

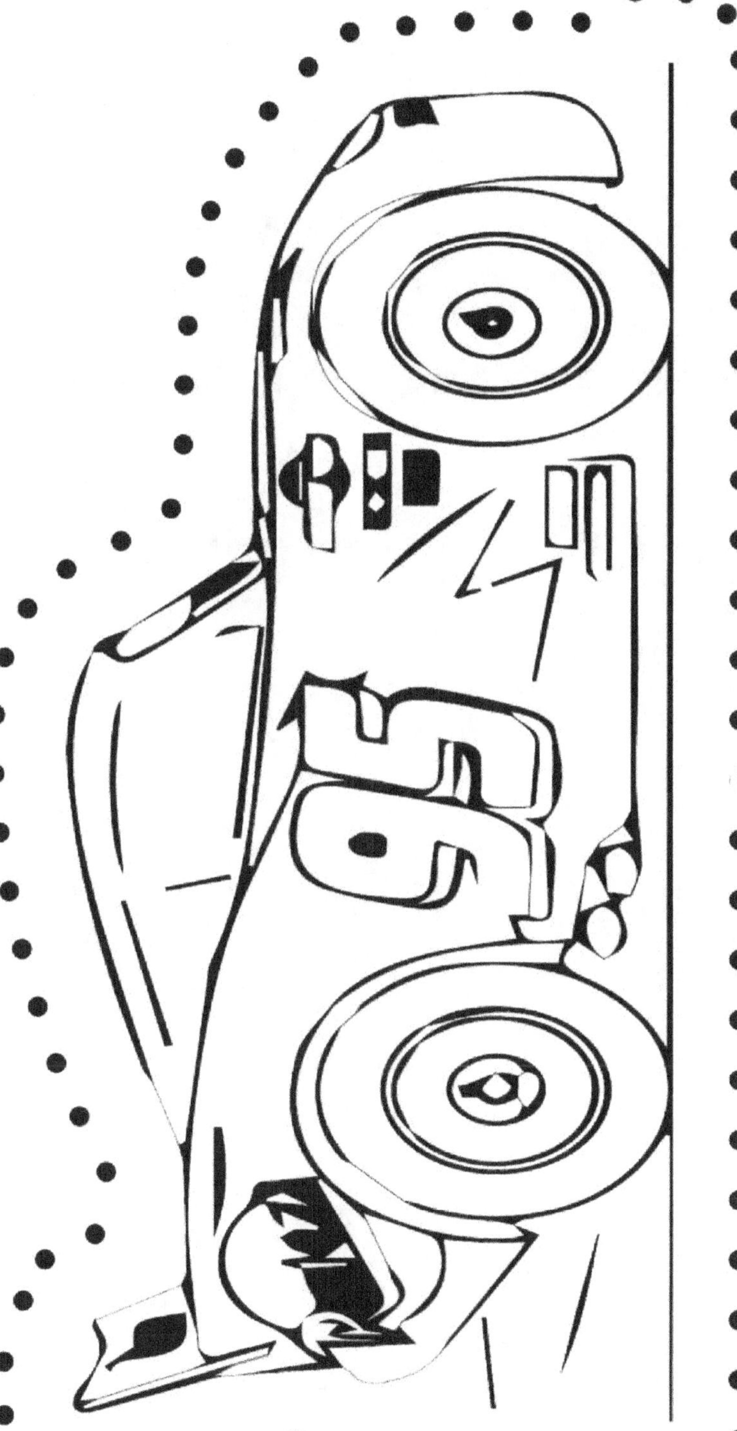

Let's cut
Color & Glue

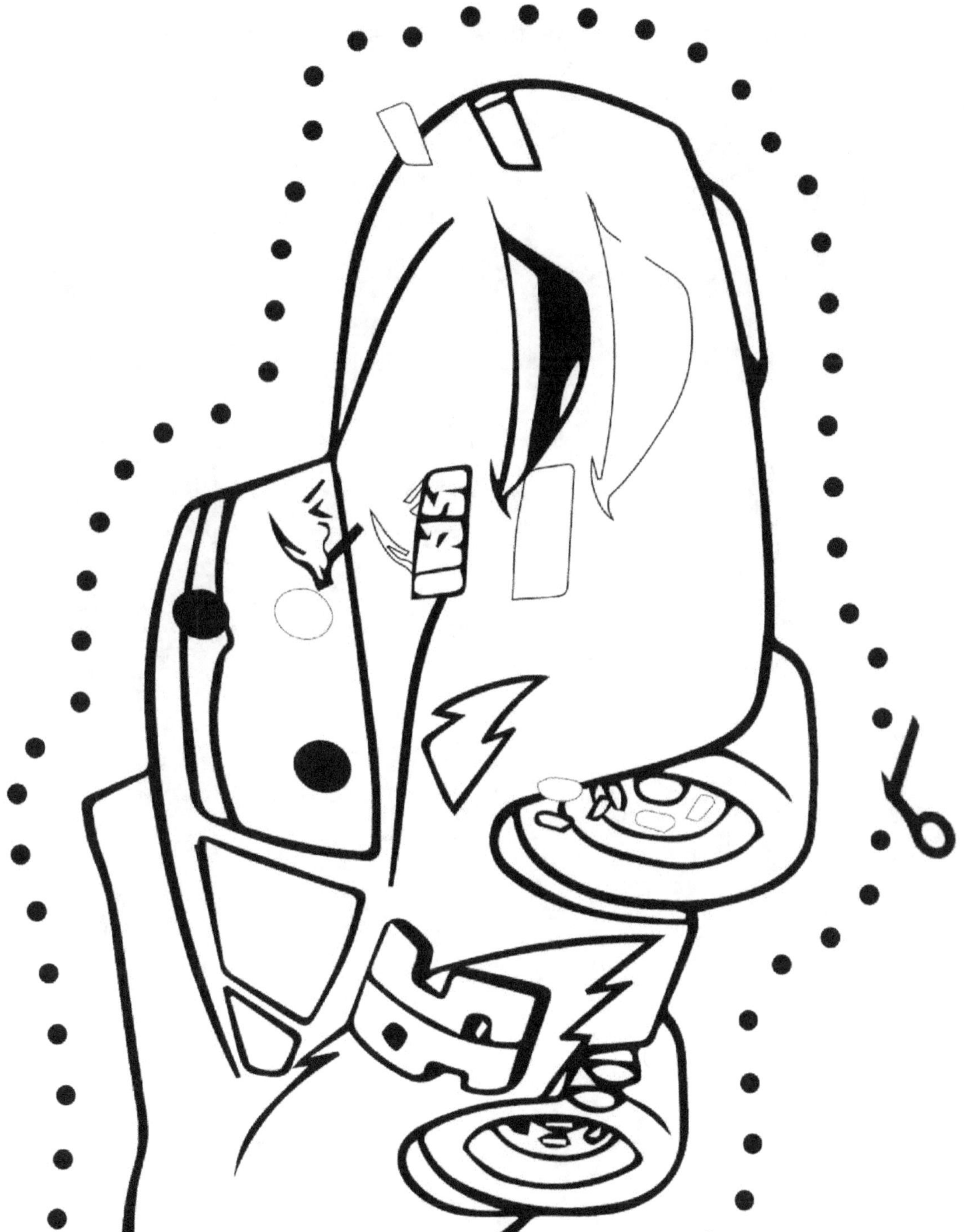

Let's cut
Color & Glue

Let's cut
Color & Glue

Let's cut
Color & Glue

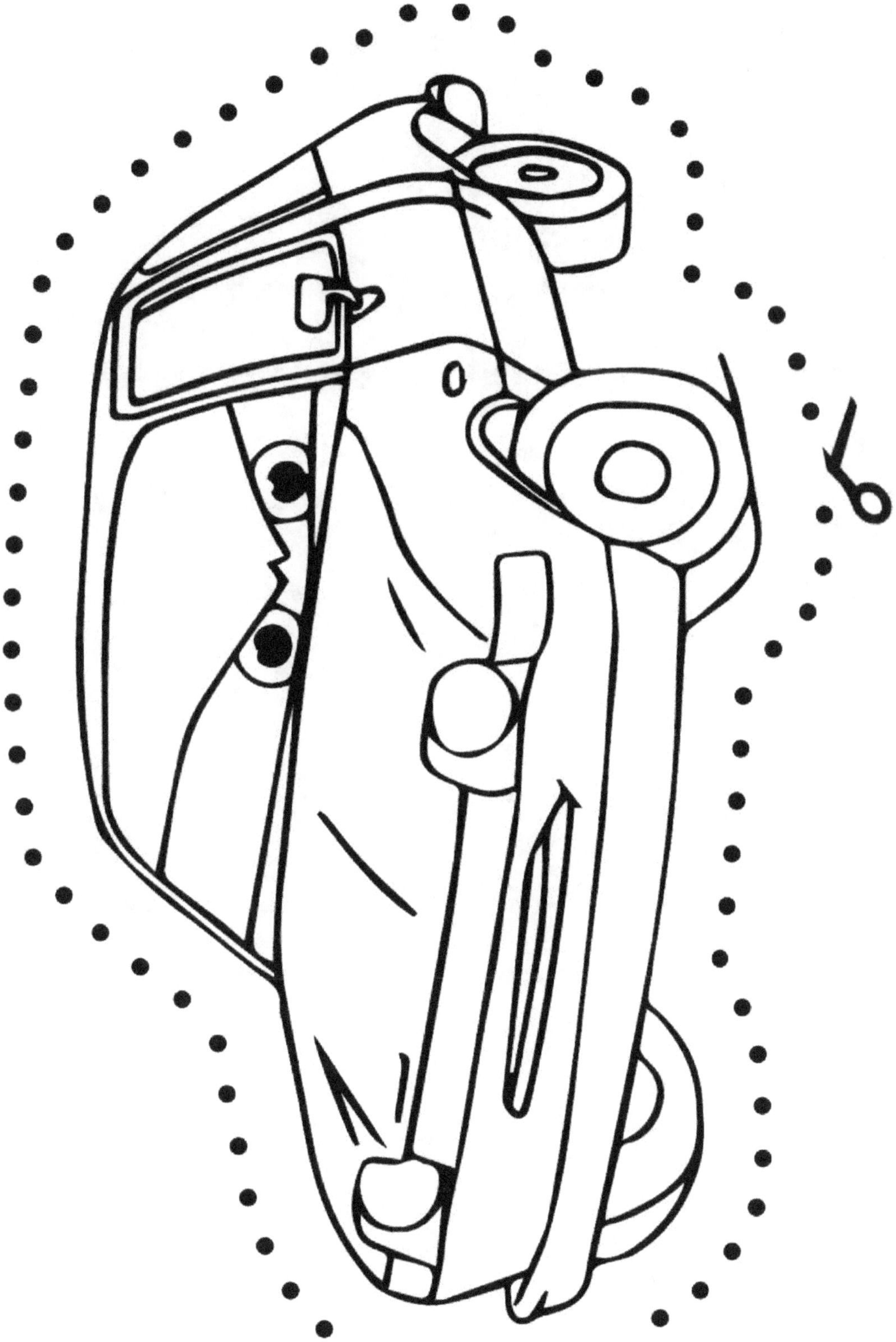

Let's cut
Color & Glue

Let's cut
Color & Glue

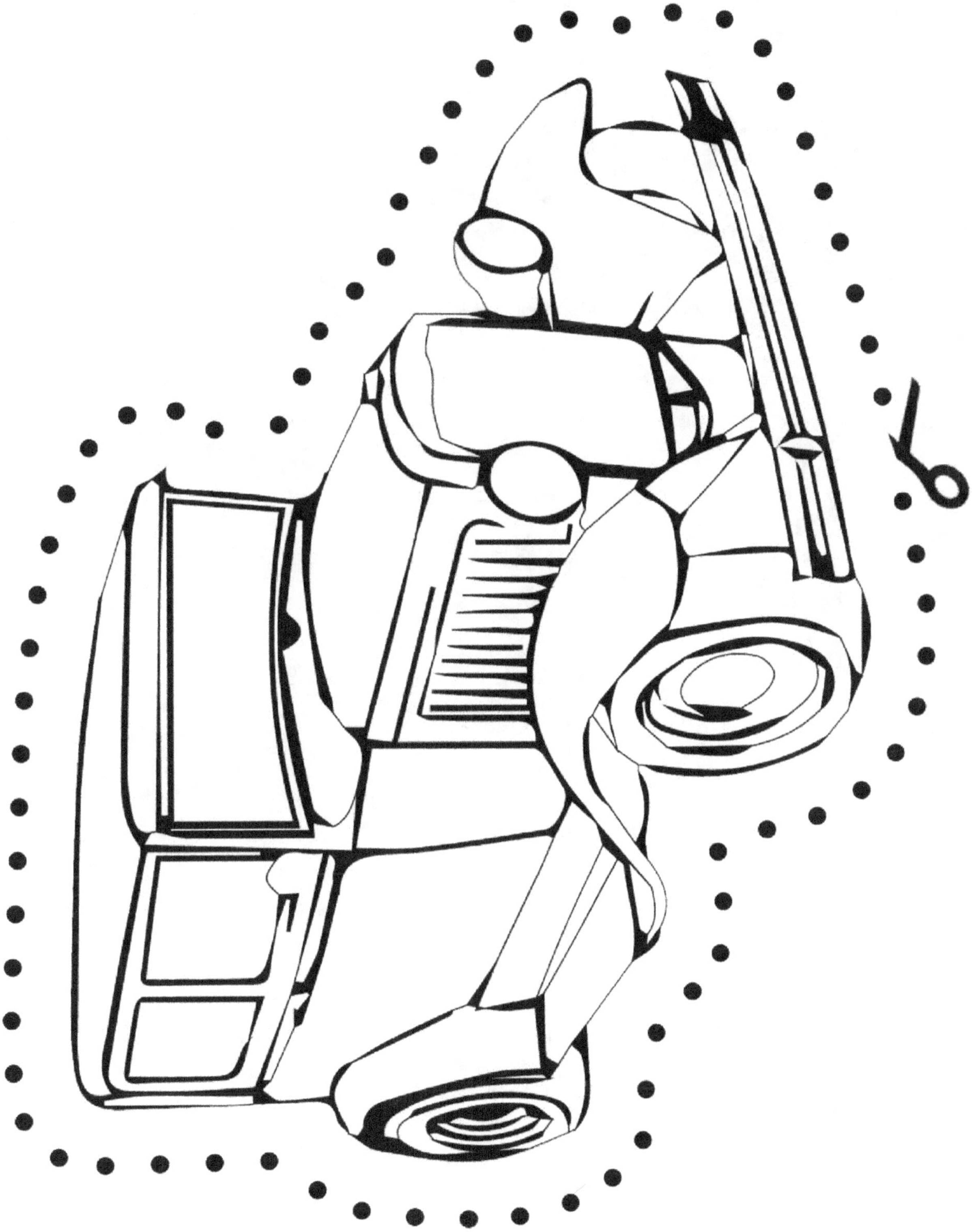

Let's cut
Color & Glue

POLICE
Let's cut
Color & Glue

POLICE

Let's cut
Color & Glue

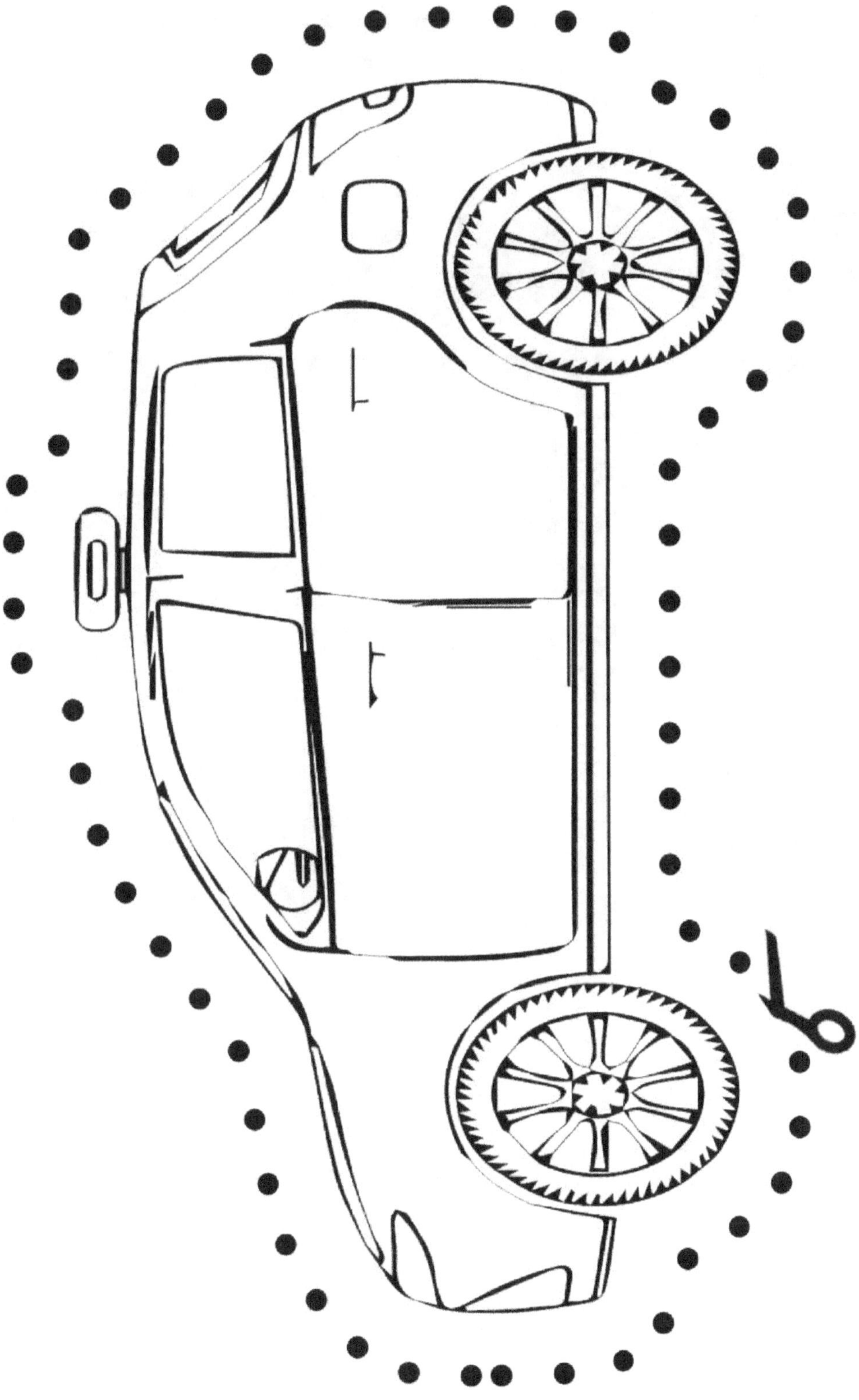

Let's cut

Let's cut
Color & Glue
POLICE

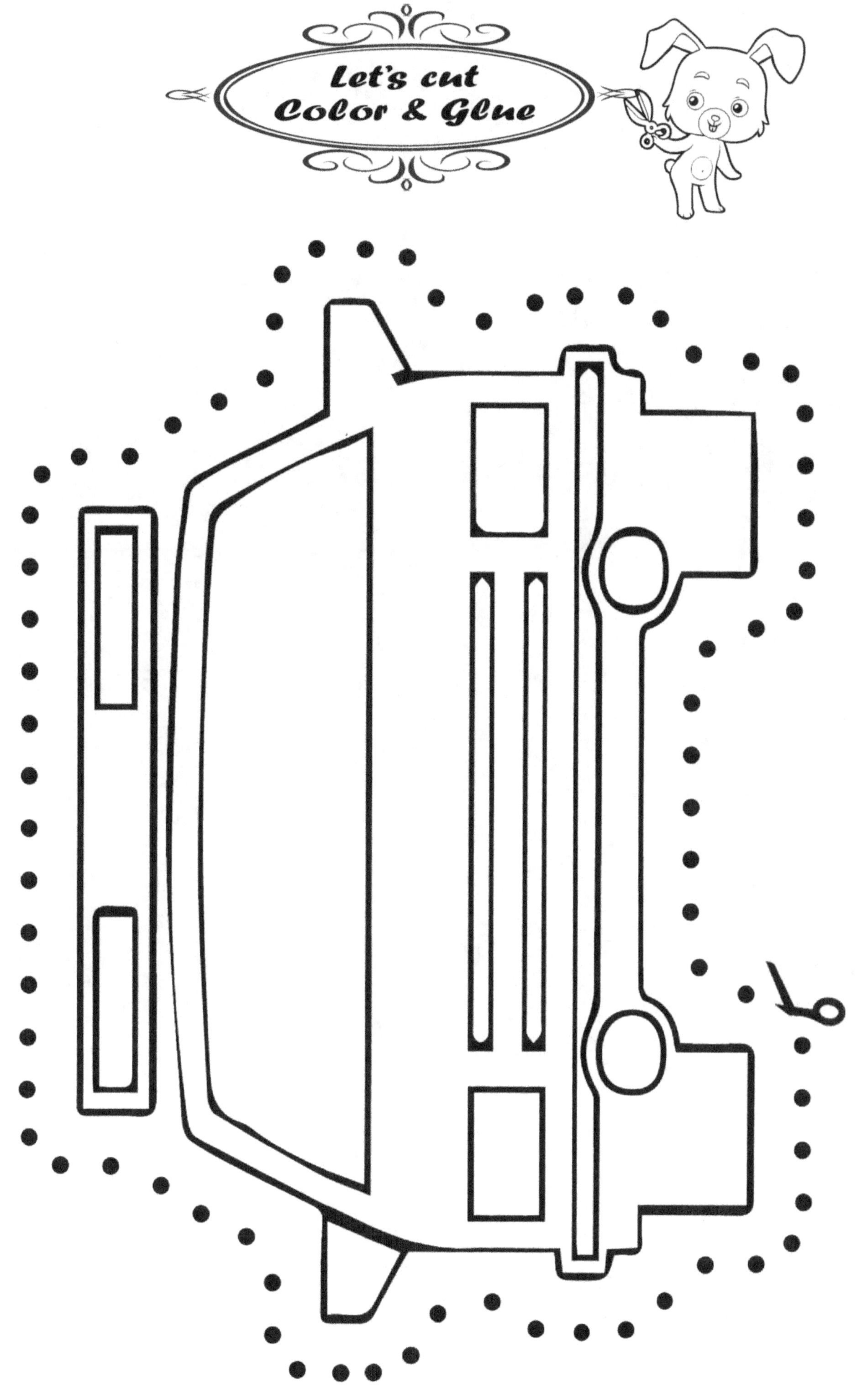

Let's cut
Color & Glue

Let's cut
Color & Glue

POLICE

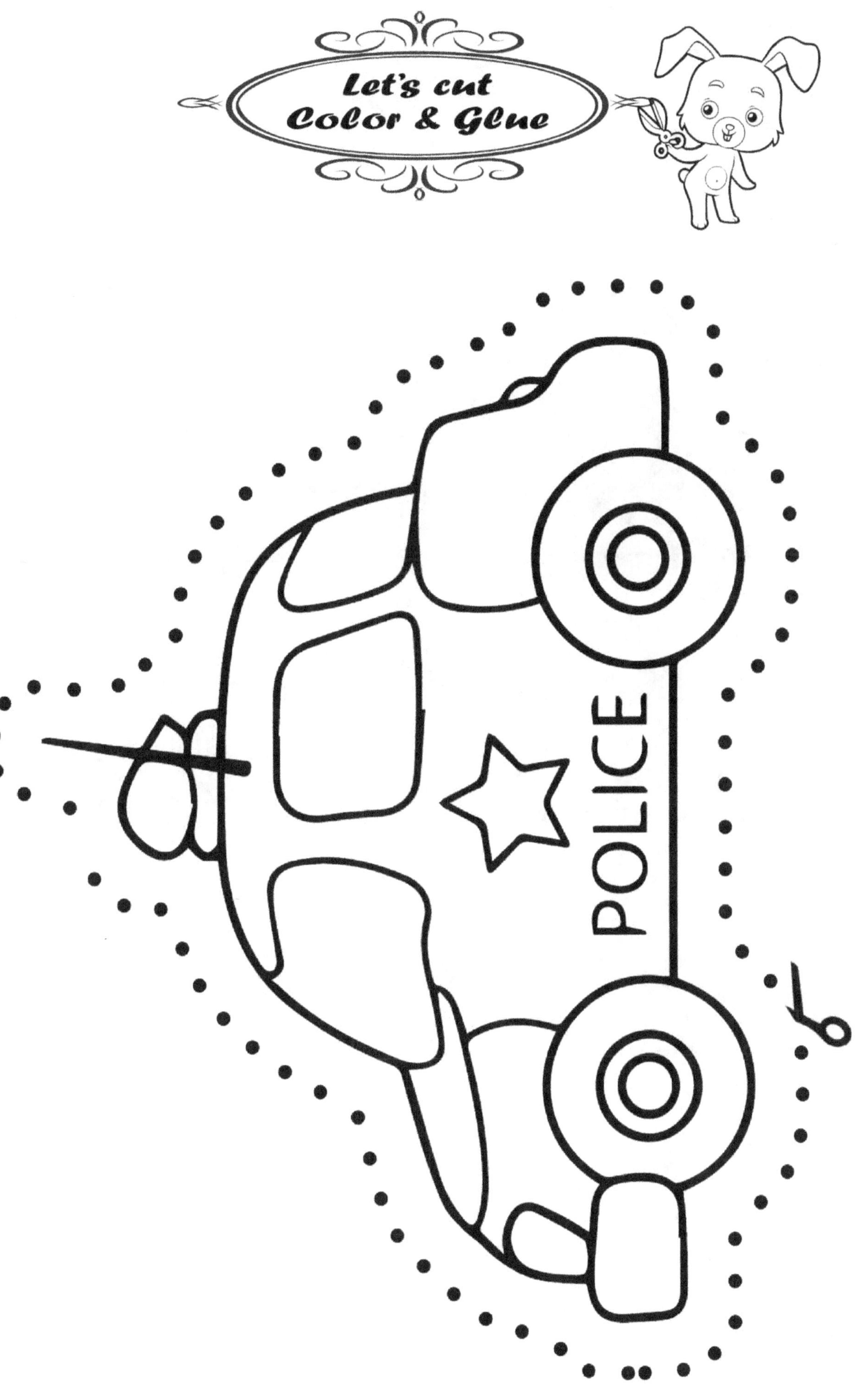

Let's cut
Color & Glue
POLICE

Let's cut
Color & Glue

POLICE
911

Let's cut
Color & Glue

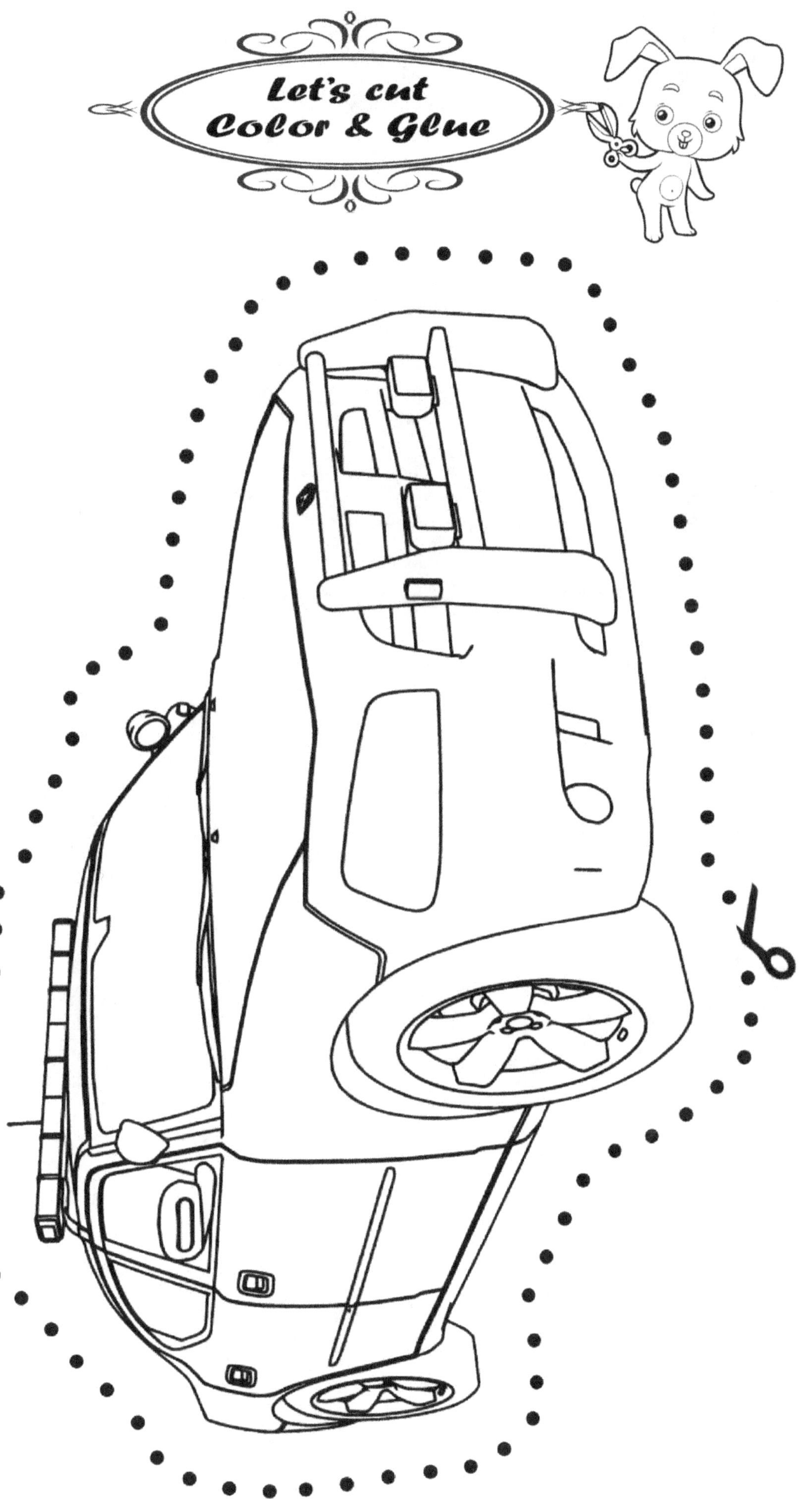

Let's cut
Color & Glue

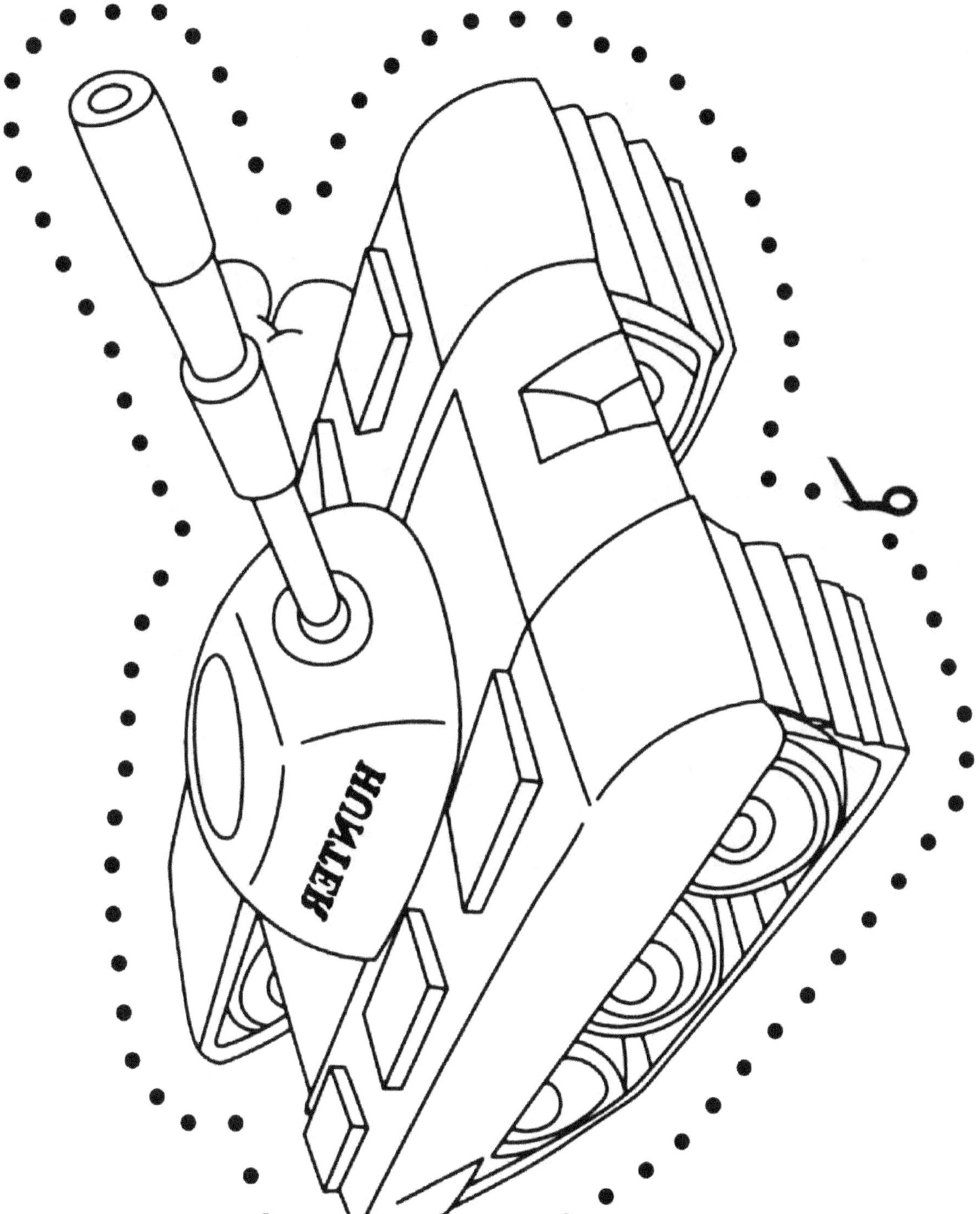

HUNTER

Let's cut

Let's cut
Color & Glue

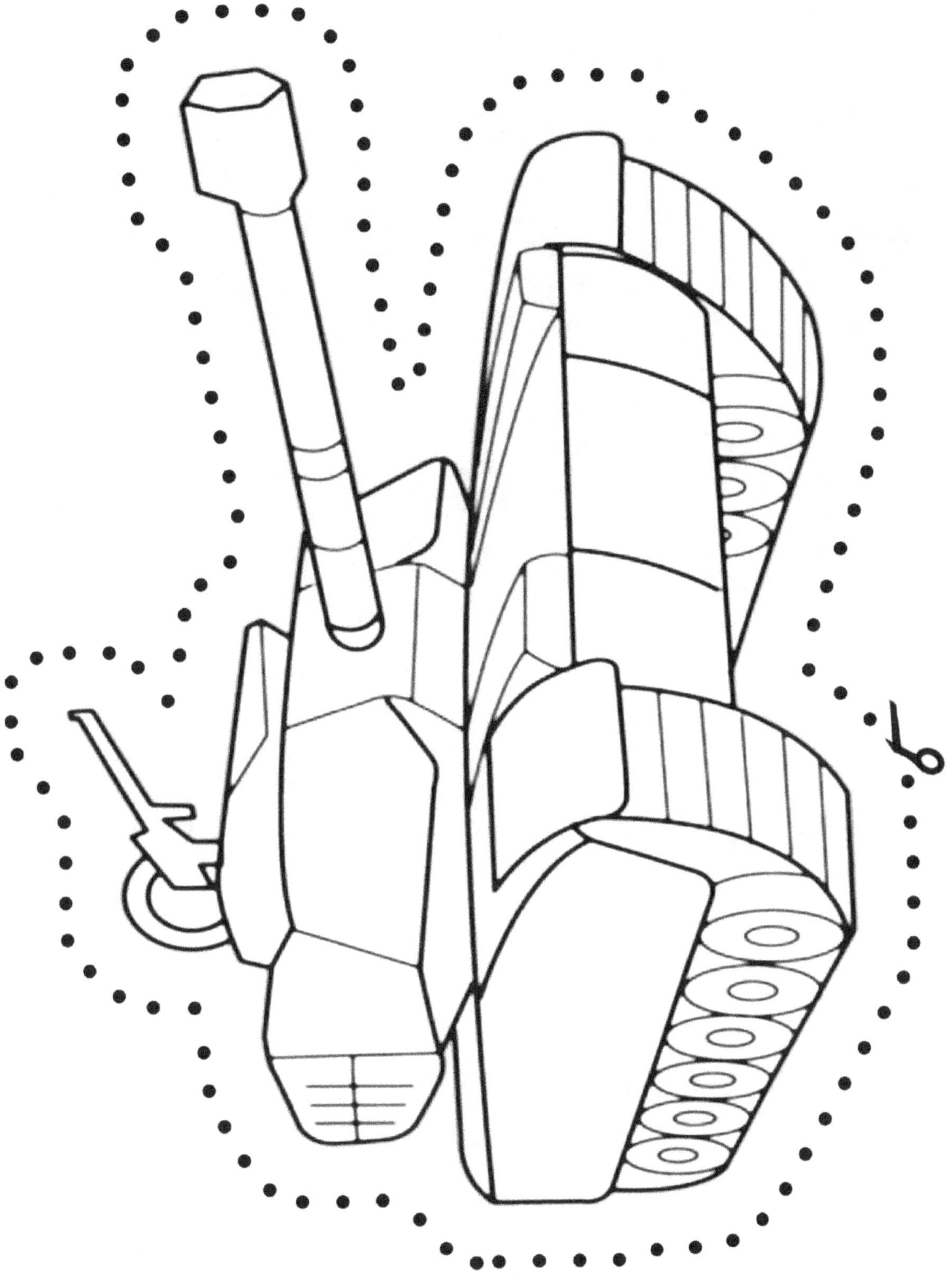

Let's cut
Color & Glue

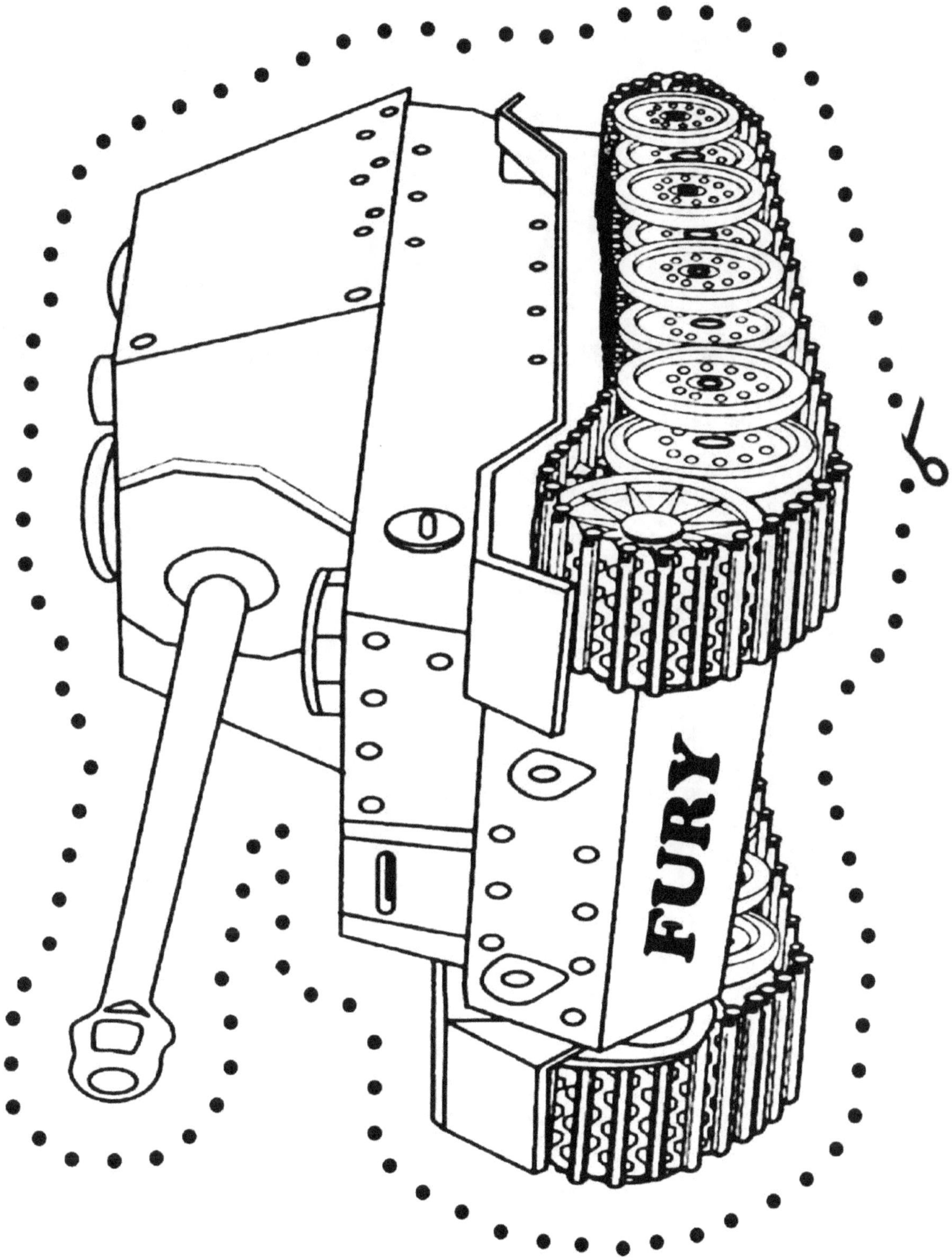

FURY

TANK

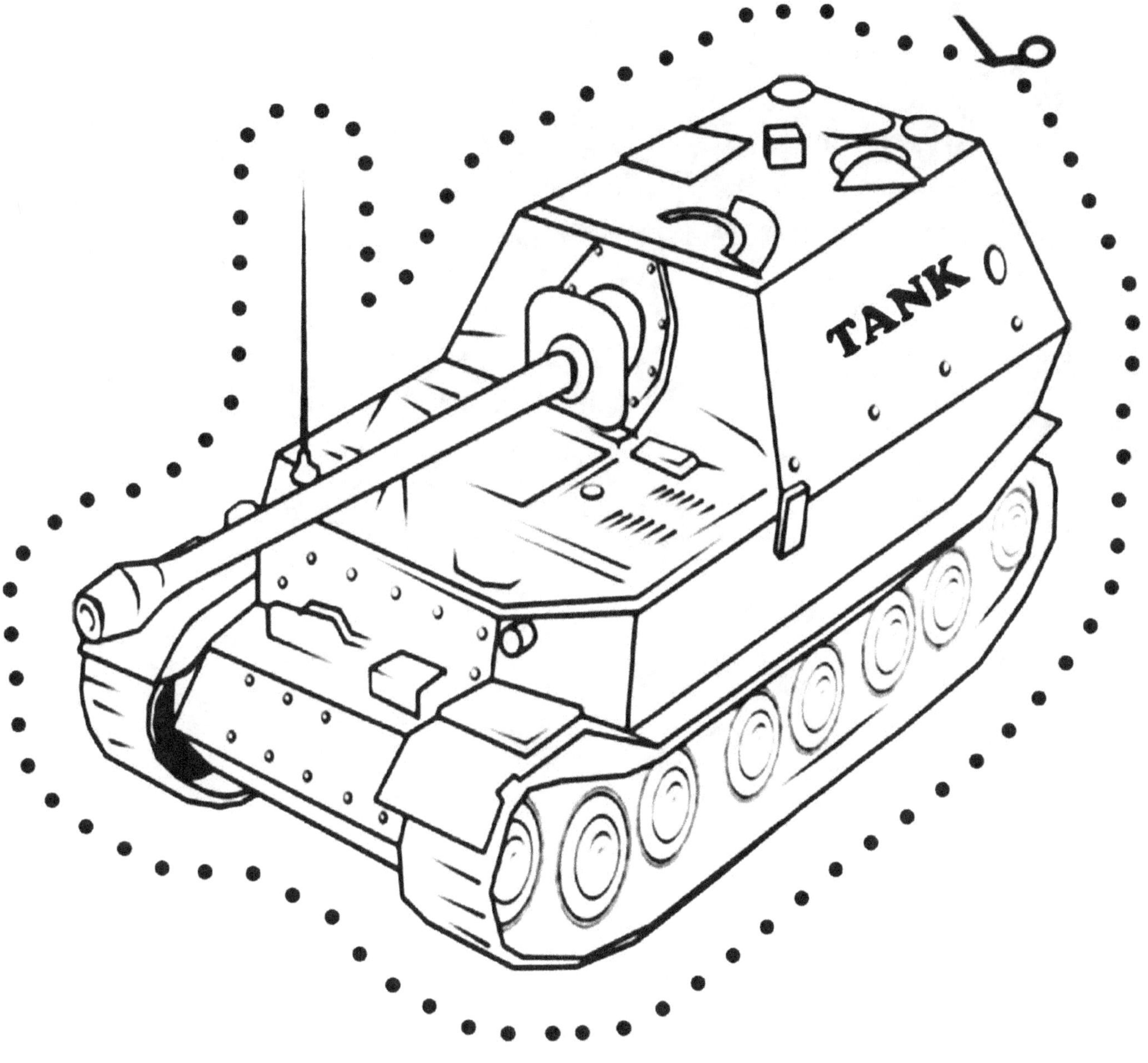

Let's cut
Color & Glue

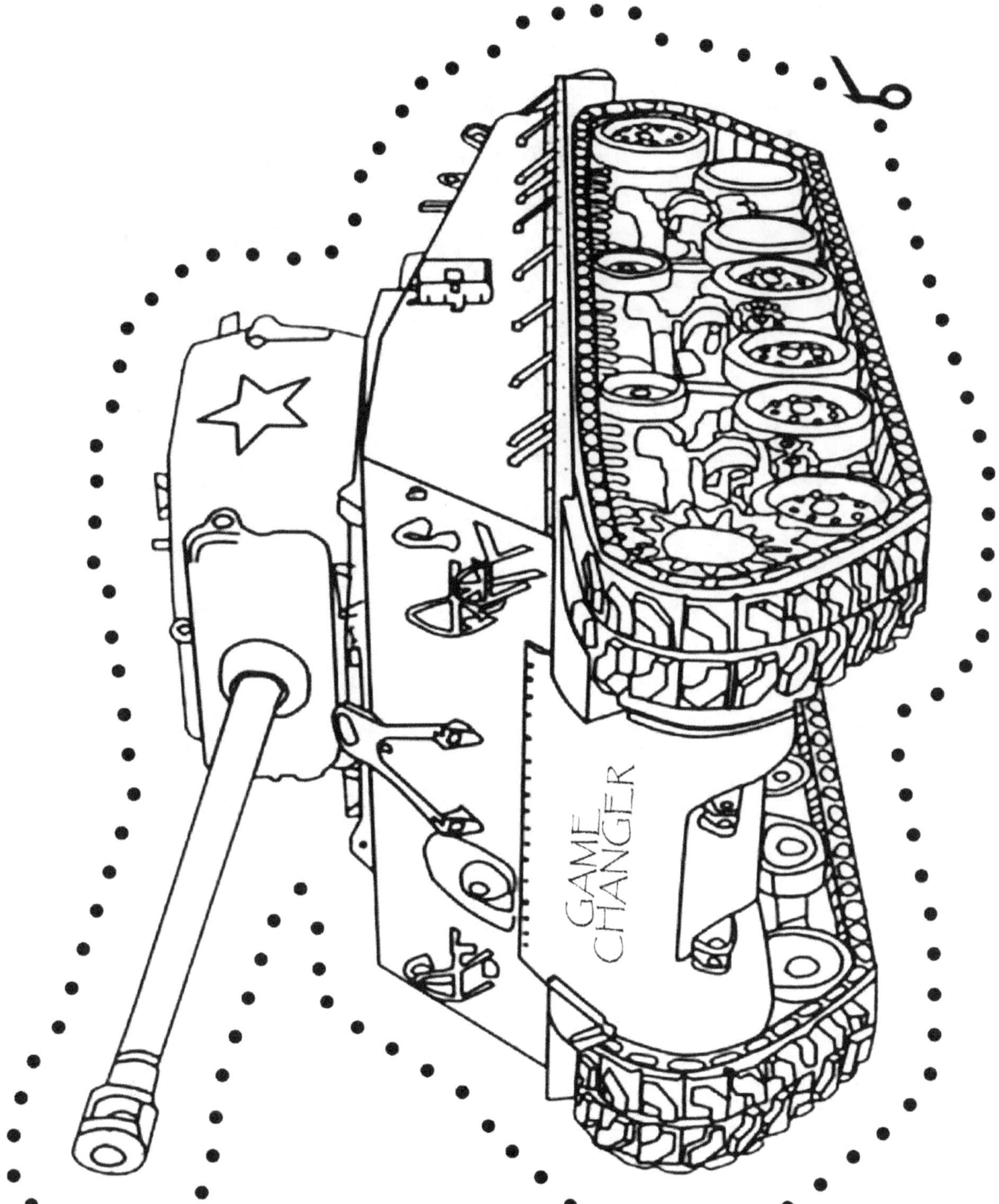

GAME
CHANGER

Let's cut
Color & Glue

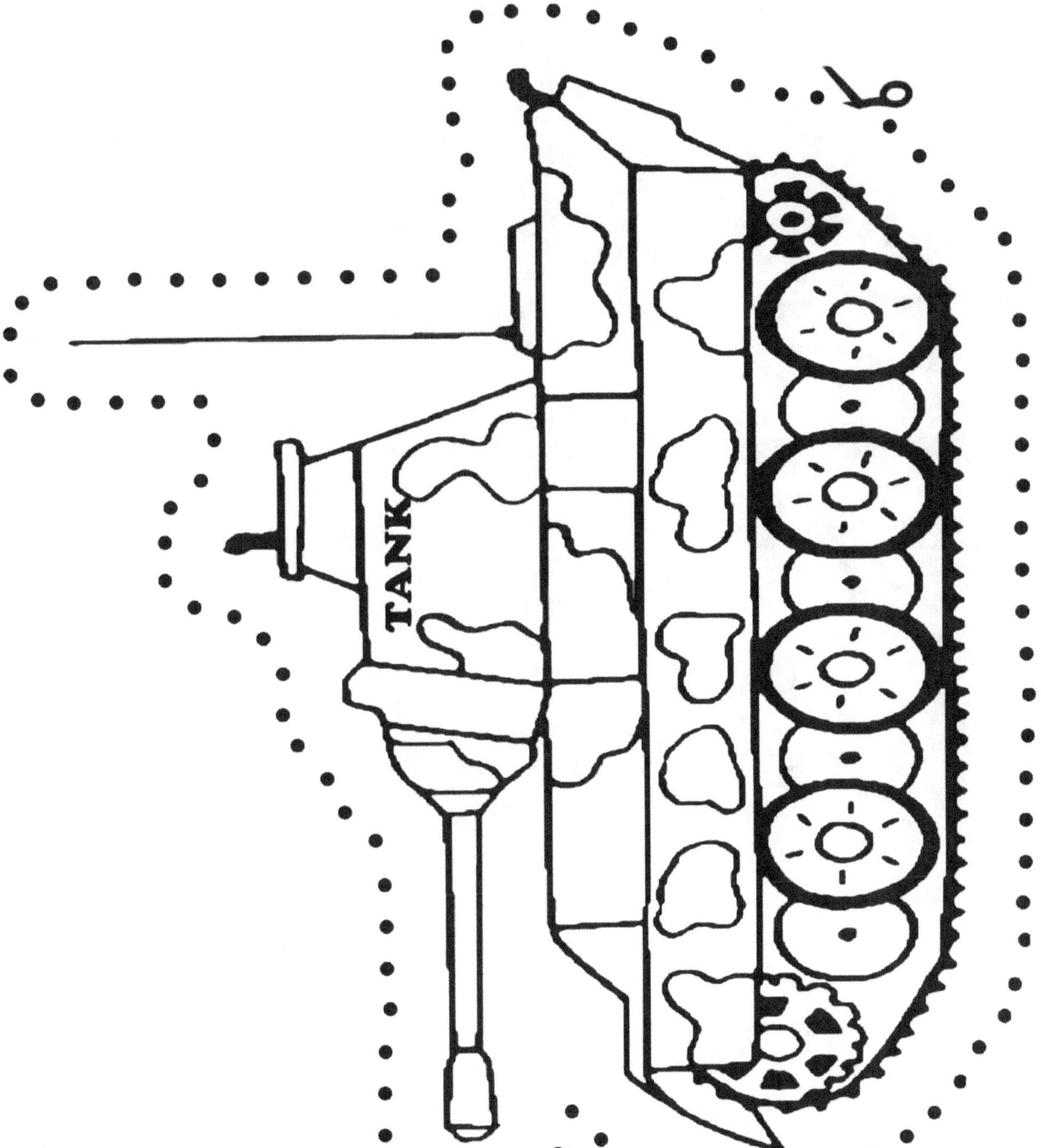

TANK

Let's cut
Color & Glue

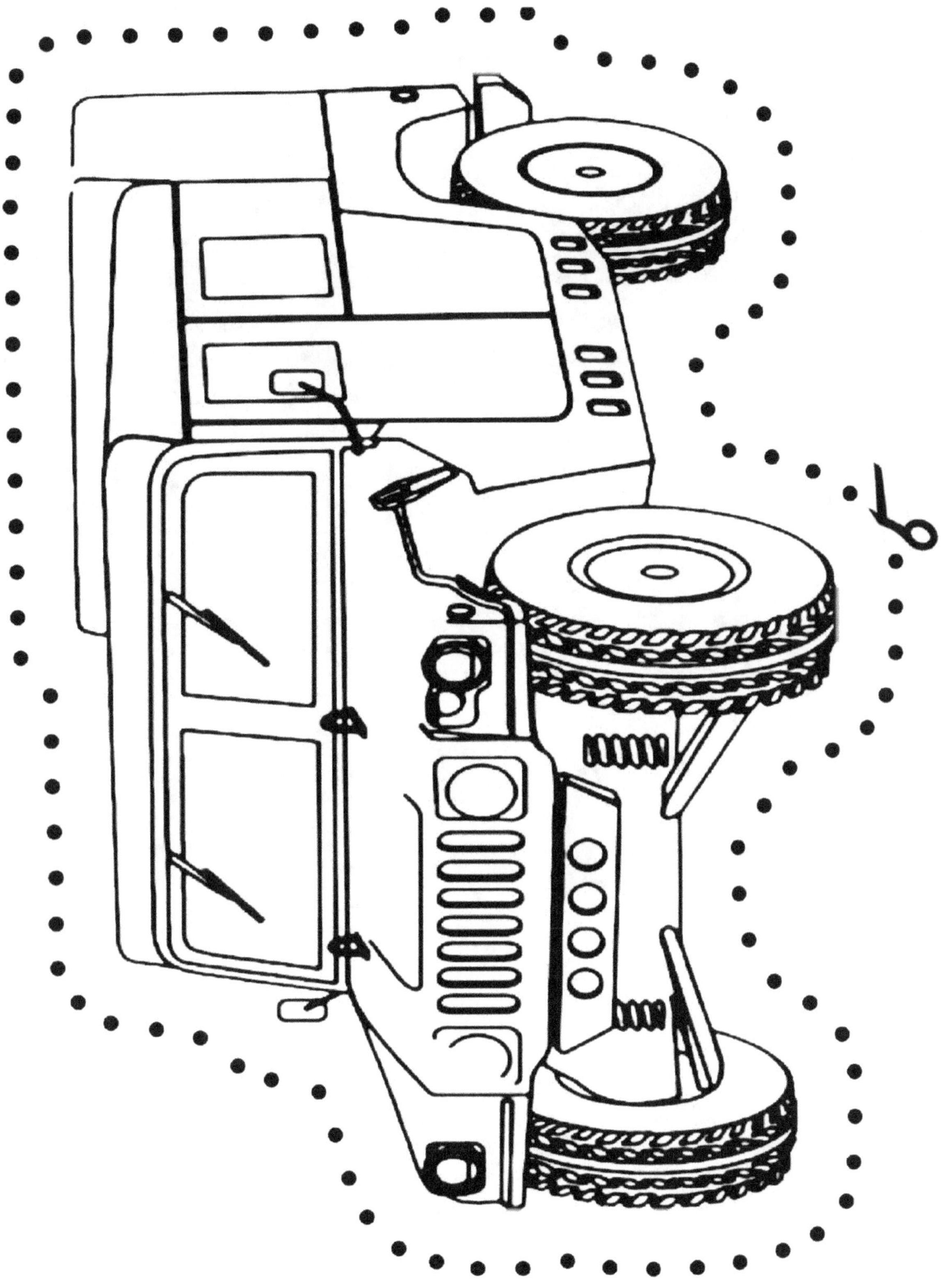

Let's cut
Color & Glue

Let's cut
Color & Glue

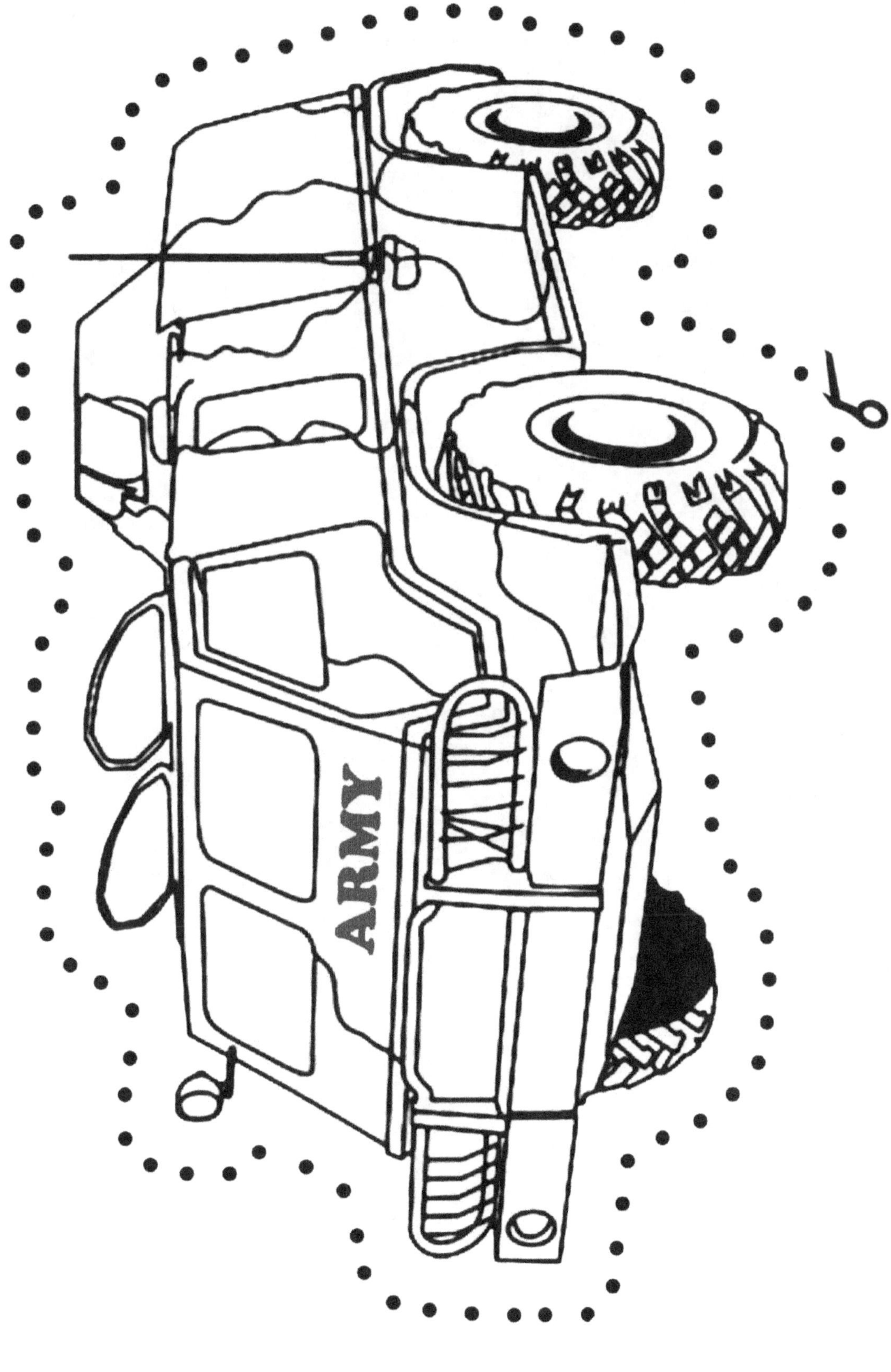

ARMY

GAM

US ARMY

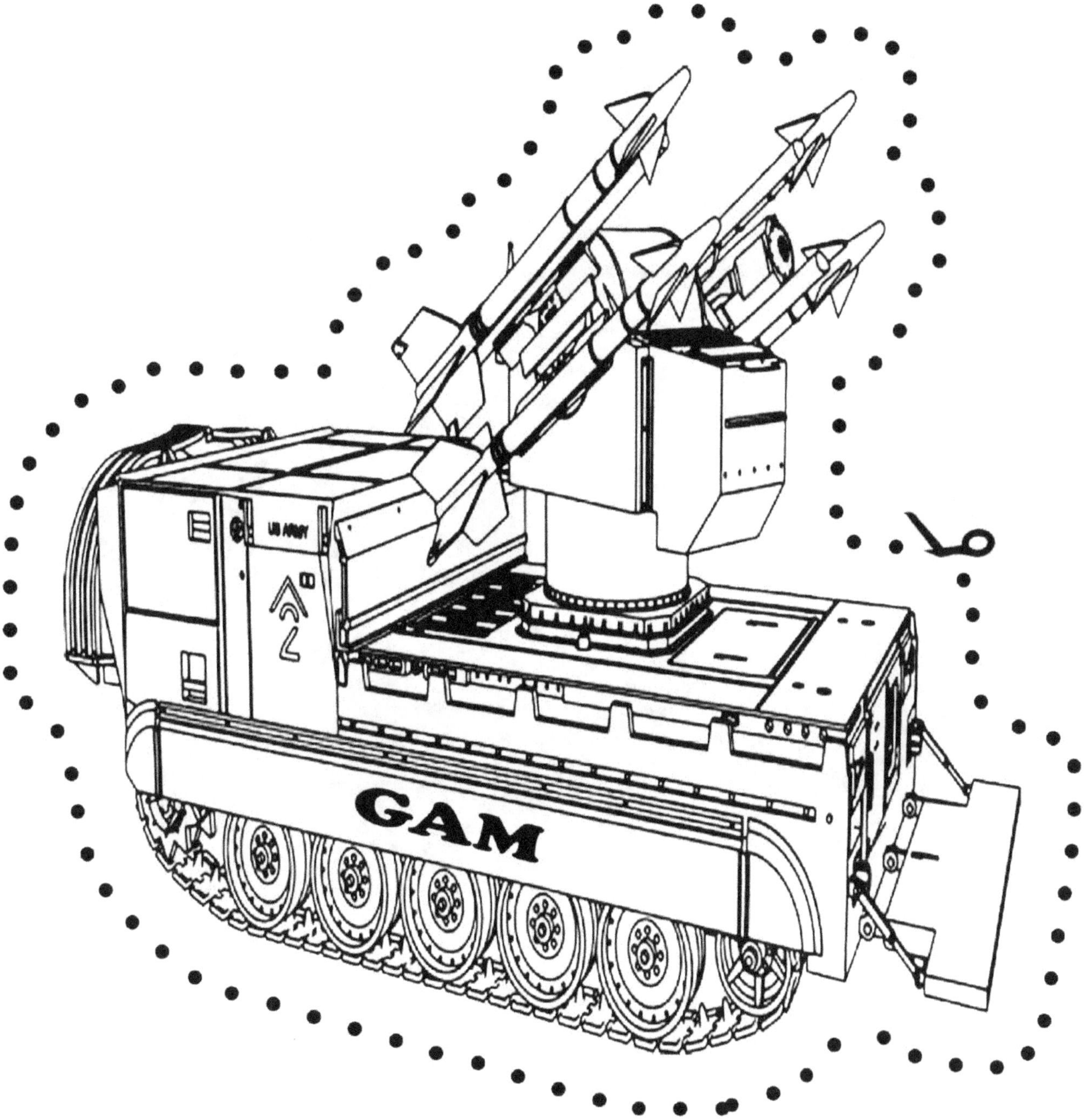

Let's cut
Color & Glue

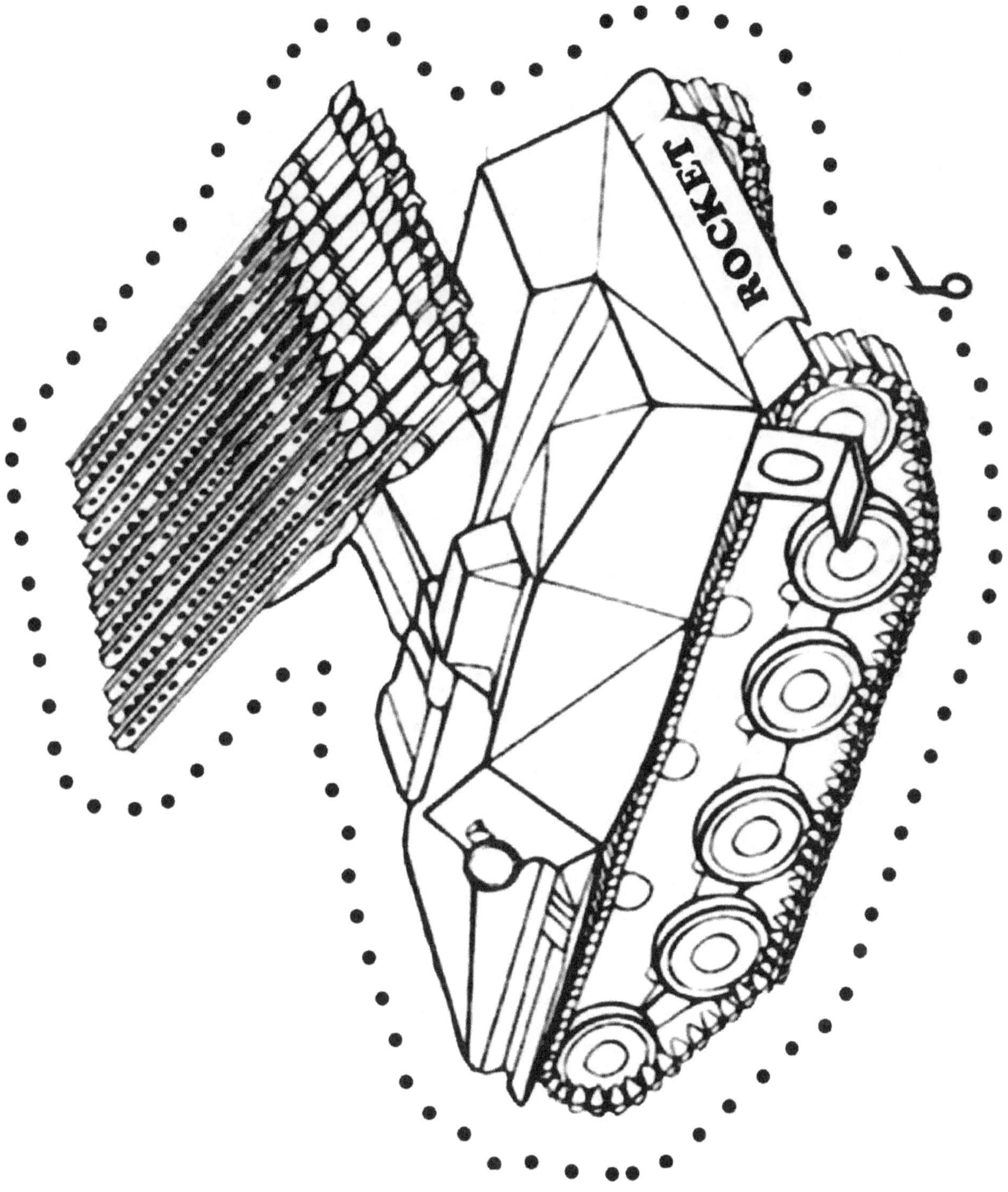

ROCKET

Let's cut
Color & Glue

School
Bus

Let's cut
Color & Glue

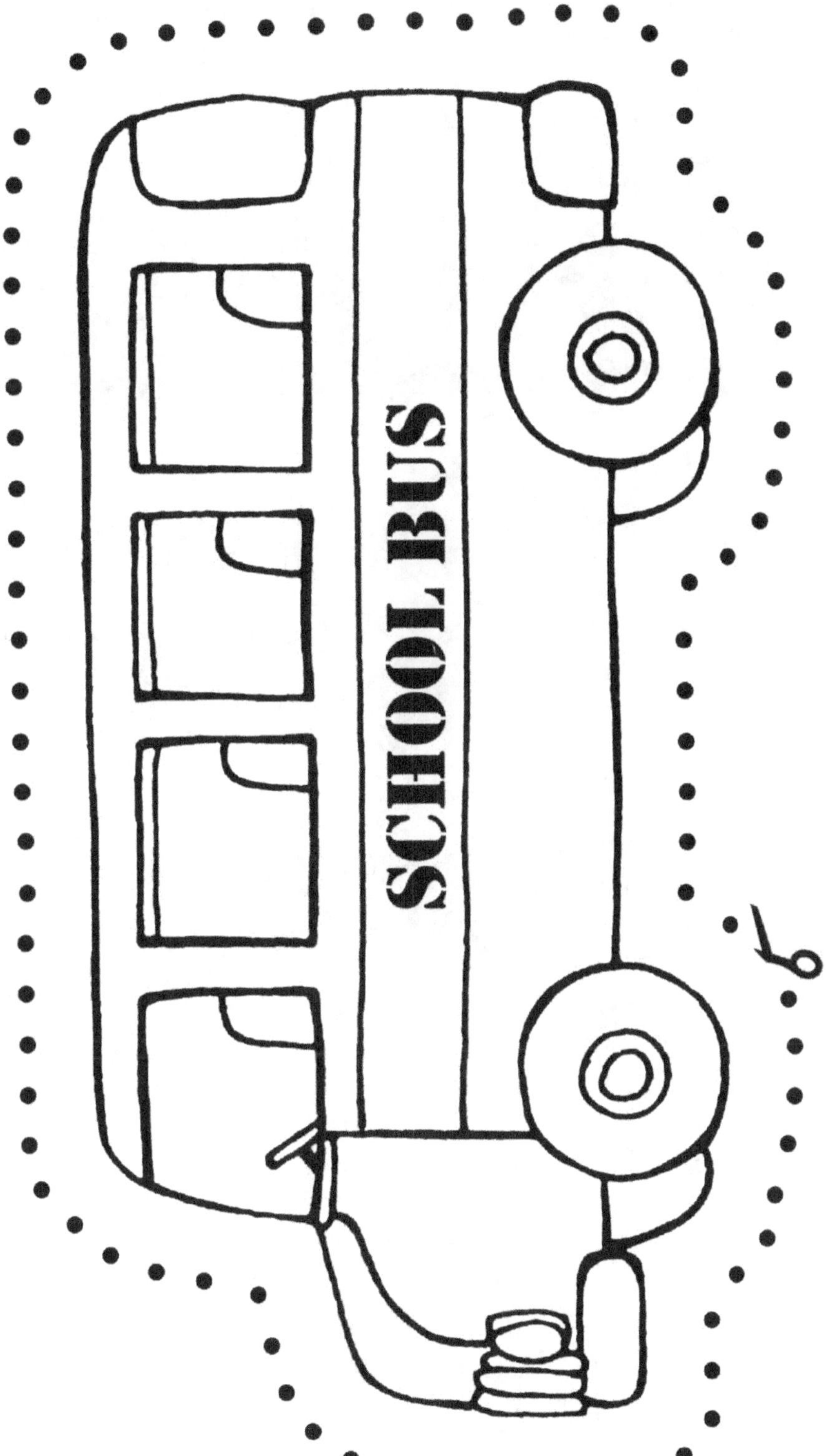

SCHOOL BUS

Let's cut
Color & Glue

Let's cut
Color & Glue

School bus